TOWARD AN AMERICAN ORTHODOX CHURCH

Toward an American Orthodox Church

by
Alexander A. Bogolepov

Foreword by
John H. Erickson

ST VLADIMIR'S SEMINARY PRESS
CRESTWOOD, NEW YORK
2001

Library of Congress Cataloging-in-Publication Data

Bogolepov, Aleksandr A. (Aleksandr Aleksandrovich), b. 1886.
    Toward an American Orthodox Church: the establishment of an
autocephalous church.
        p.   cm.
    Includes bibliographical references ans index.
    ISBN 0-88141-227-9 (alk. paper)
    1. Orthodox Eastern Church—Government.   2. Canon law, Orthodox
Eastern.   3. Metropolitanates.   I. Title.
    LAW
    262'.019—dc21

                                                          2001019524

Revised 2001 by
St Vladimir's Seminary Press
575 Scarsdale Rd., Crestwood NY 10707
1-800-204-2665

ISBN 0-88141-227-9

Two of the cover images merit further note. The photograph in the bottom right
hand corner was taken at the canonization of Bishop Raphael of Brooklyn, in
the year 2000—the first Orthodox saint canonized on American soil. The center
photograph at the top is of an Orthodox church on Kodiak Island, Alaska. Both
photographs courtesy of the archives of the Orthodox Church in America. All
other photographs taken by Jenny Schroedel or Amber Houx.

Toward an American Orthodox Church

by
Alexander A. Bogolepov

Foreword by
John H. Erickson

ST VLADIMIR'S SEMINARY PRESS
CRESTWOOD, NEW YORK
2001

Library of Congress Cataloging-in-Publication Data

Bogolepov, Aleksandr A. (Aleksandr Aleksandrovich), b. 1886.
　　Toward an American Orthodox Church: the establishment of an
　　autocephalous church.
　　　　p.　cm.
　　Includes bibliographical references ans index.
　　ISBN 0-88141-227-9 (alk. paper)
　　1. Orthodox Eastern Church—Government.　2. Canon law, Orthodox
　　Eastern.　3. Metropolitanates.　I. Title.
　　LAW
　　262'.019—dc21

2001019524

Revised 2001 by
St Vladimir's Seminary Press
575 Scarsdale Rd., Crestwood NY 10707
1-800-204-2665

ISBN 0-88141-227-9

Two of the cover images merit further note. The photograph in the bottom right hand corner was taken at the canonization of Bishop Raphael of Brooklyn, in the year 2000—the first Orthodox saint canonized on American soil. The center photograph at the top is of an Orthodox church on Kodiak Island, Alaska. Both photographs courtesy of the archives of the Orthodox Church in America. All other photographs taken by Jenny Schroedel or Amber Houx.

Acknowledgment

The publication of this book has been underwritten by a grant provided by the Orthodox Christian Laity (OCL). OCL is a voluntary independent movement of laity and clergy, founded in 1987, concerned with the well-being of the Orthodox Christian Church and the laity's legitimate role in church governance. It is dedicated to syndiaconia *(co-ministry) of clergy and laity; spiritual renewal and education; and as a priority advocates the establishment of a united and self-governing church in the United States.*

ORTHODOX CHRISTIAN LAITY

30 North LaSalle Street • Suite 4020 • Chicago, IL 60602-2513
Fax: 312-332-4905 • E-mail: ocl.adm@ocl.org • Website: http://www.ocl.org

Contents

FOREWORD

The Orthodox Church is a communion or family of sister local churches, united in faith, sacramental life and canonical order, but in other respects fully self-governing, *i.e.,* "autocephalous" (lit. "self-headed"), having the capacity to manage their own affairs and select their own bishops, including the "primate" or head of the church, without necessary recourse to another church. In principle at least, Orthodox ecclesiology therefore aims at "unity in plurality," and in this respect it differs from both Protestant ecclesiology (which could be characterized as "disunity in plurality") and from older Roman Catholic ecclesiology ("unity without plurality"). Over the centuries, this ecclesiological understanding has allowed Orthodoxy to adapt to new circumstances and to become deeply embedded in a variety of cultural contexts, from its traditional Old World bastions in the Eastern Mediterranean, the Balkans and Russia to the native villages of Alaska. But in the modern world, this ecclesiology has faced new challenges. Communist domination in much of Eastern Europe during the twentieth century severely restricted the churches' freedom. Nationalism has encouraged subordination of the churches to ethnic or state interests. Massive emigration to America and other new lands has created the unprecedented situation of multiple "diasporas," with ties of varying strength to ecclesiastical centers in the Old World, coexisting on the same territory. As a result, the problem of how a new local church is to be established has become a critical one for contemporary Orthodoxy.

When Professor Alexander A. Bogolepov's *Toward an American Orthodox Church* first appeared in 1963, this problem was already being discussed at various levels of church life. In America, ordinary parishioners were tiring of inter-jurisdictional disputes and litigation, and they were becoming increasingly aware of a common Orthodox identity that transcended their ethnic differences. In addition, the newly-formed Standing Conference of Canonical Orthodox Bishops in America (SCOBA) was taking tentative steps toward the structural unity of Orthodoxy in America.[1] On a world level, the First Pan-Orthodox Conference at Rhodes in 1961 tentatively placed the issues of autocephaly, autonomy and the "diaspora" on the agenda of a forthcoming Great and Holy Council. Professor Bogolepov's book gave both seriousness and direction to the discussion of such issues. A former professor of law in Russia and later professor of canon law at St Vladimir's Seminary, Bogolepov was well acquainted not only with the ancient canons of the Church but also with the wide range of historical circumstances in which these have been applied—and sometimes misapplied. But in addition to being a serious scholarly study, *Toward an American Orthodox Church*— as its title suggests—envisions the establishment of a local church in America which, while remaining fully Orthodox, would be fully self-governing and thus relatively free from

1   A useful historical study of SCOBA initiatives during the 1960s as well as of other important aspects of our subject is presented in Archimandrite Serafim [Surrency], *The Quest for Orthodox Church Unity in America* (New York: Saints Boris and Gleb Press, 1973). A more popular account is presented in John H. Erickson, *Orthodox Christians in America* (New York and Oxford: Oxford University Press, 1999), 113-15 et passim.

the various pressures and political entanglements of the "mother churches" in the Old World.

In his book, Professor Bogolepov advocates pan-Orthodox involvement and consensus in the establishment of a new local church. Perhaps with a note of wishful thinking, he writes:

> As practice has evolved, the recognition of a new Church and its introduction into the community of Orthodox Local Churches is now decided not by one Mother Church nor by the Ecumenical Patriarch in Constantinople alone, but by all the autocephalous Local Churches together. They reserve the right to accept or disapprove the decision of the Mother Church or the Ecumenical Patriarch... From the jurisdiction of a single Local Church this problem is coming to be decided by all the Local Churches, and thus the ancient principle of deciding this matter by the whole community of autocephalous Churches is being revived. (p. 46)

But in the 1960s, pan-Orthodox consensus was in short supply. Despite appeals from SCOBA, the issue of Orthodox structural unity in America was not taken up at a Pan-Orthodox Conference. Indeed, when the Fourth Pan-Orthodox Conference met near Geneva in 1968 to finalize an agenda for the projected Great and Holy Council, it did not even include the issues of autocephaly, autonomy and the "diaspora," even though these had been among the issues previously recommended for inclusion by the First Pan-Orthodox Conference in 1961. Inter-Orthodox tensions—particularly between the Russian Orthodox Church and the Patriarchate of Constantinople—meant that the projected council's agenda would be limited to "safe" subjects and would avoid such controversial subjects as the future of Orthodoxy in America.

One reason for these tensions was the unsettled relationship between the Russian Orthodox Church—Moscow Patriarchate and various groups of Russian background in America and elsewhere that had separated from the Russian Orthodox Church in the tumultuous years following the Communist Revolution in 1917.[2] So critical was this complex subject by the 1960s that Professor Bogolepov devotes two long chapters, comprising nearly half his book, to it, one to the Russian Orthodox Church Abroad (also known as the Russian Orthodox Church Outside Russia or the Synod) and one to the Russian Orthodox Greek Catholic Church of America (the former North American Metropolitanate of the Russian Orthodox Church, more commonly known simply as the Metropolia). In the 1920s and 1930s, the church in Russia had been pushed to the brink of total liquidation. During World War II, however, the church had helped to rally the Russian people in support of the war effort, and in return Stalin ended efforts to exterminate the faith by sheer force. The church was allowed to function, but only under close government supervision. Church buildings were reopened for worship. New patriarchal elections were held. This revival of the Russian Orthodox Church within the Soviet Union made it hard for other Orthodox churches to continue to ignore it or to question its legitimacy. By the 1960s, assisted by the other Orthodox churches of Soviet-dominated Eastern Europe, the Russian Orthodox Church was playing an increasingly active role in Orthodox affairs, *e.g.*, in the Great and Holy Council project. At the same time, it was pressuring the Patriarchate of

2   For a somewhat fuller presentation of what follows, see Erickson, *Orthodox Christians*, 115-19.

Constantinople and the other autocephalous Orthodox churches to end their *de facto* recognition of groups in the West that it regarded as schismatic.

Of these groups, the Metropolia, unlike the Russian Orthodox Church Outside Russia, was willing to recognize the revived Moscow Patriarchate as legitimate and to establish normal relations with it. The *de facto* independence that the Metropolia had enjoyed since the 1920s was originally intended to be a temporary measure until a future council of the Russian Orthodox Church could deal with ecclesiastical affairs "under conditions of political freedom." But had that time arrived? Many members of the Metropolia, Professor Bogolepov among them, feared that submission to the Moscow Patriarchate would compromise the Metropolia's internal freedom and limit its ability to speak out against continuing religious oppression in the Soviet Union and elsewhere. In addition, they valued the full participation of all the faithful—laity as well as bishops and other clergy—at all levels of their church life. Such participation—so characteristic of the early church—had been mandated in modern times by the All-Russian Church Council (Sobor) held in Moscow in 1917-18. But as Professor Bogolepov forcefully argues, the principles of the Moscow Council were faithfully maintained only by the Metropolia. "The Russian Orthodox Church in the Soviet Union, under the rule of the Communist government, simply had no opportunity to adhere to these principles," while the Russian Orthodox Church Outside Russia "repudiated the conciliar cooperation of the clergy and laity which was established by the 1917 Sobor" (p. 111). But an additional reason must be given for the Metropolia's reluctance to relinquish its independence. By the 1960s, many in the Metropolia no longer regarded themselves as part of a "Russian" jurisdiction. Their church had assumed an increasingly American character. A growing percentage of its membership were converts, and the vast majority of its "cradle Orthodox" spoke only English. They looked forward to the establishment of the kind of American Orthodox Church that Professor Bogolepov wrote of.

Discussion of autocephaly took a new turn in 1970. In line with the policy of peaceful coexistence then prevailing in Soviet-American relations, the Russian Orthodox Church softened its earlier stance towards the Metropolia. The North American "daughter church" was reconciled with its Russian "mother church," and in turn the Russian Orthodox Church granted the Metropolia autocephaly as the Orthodox Church in America (OCA). While this resolved the old problem of the Metropolia's relationship to the Russian Orthodox Church, it created a new problem. The Patriarchate of Constantinople, together with the other Greek-led churches (Alexandria, Jerusalem, Cyprus and Greece), refused to recognize the Metropolia's new status and name. On the other hand, a number of Orthodox churches in Eastern Europe did recognize the autocephaly of the OCA (Bulgaria, Poland, Czechoslovakia and Georgia), while still other churches adopted a wait-and-see attitude (Antioch, Romania and Serbia). An immediate result of this stand-off was an angry exchange of letters between the patriarchs of Moscow and Constantinople, which revealed at the highest official level the extent and depth of disagreement between these churches over a host of ecclesiological issues, not only over the status of the Metropolia/OCA but also over the status of other autocephalous and/or autonomous churches established in the course of the twentieth century (Poland, Czechoslovakia) and indeed of the Russian Orthodox Church itself.[3] This exchange was followed by controversial literature, wildly uneven in quality and tone, from both sides.[4]

The ensuing crisis presented the Orthodox churches with a new opportunity to address the question of how a new local church is to be established and, indeed, the question of the very nature of the local church. The storm of controversy surrounding the autocephaly of the OCA had the potential to become a "meaningful storm," to use the words of Fr. Alexander Schmemann, "a unique opportunity for facing and solving an ecclesiastical confusion which for too long a time was simply ignored by the Orthodox."[5] And in fact, when the First Pan-Orthodox Preconciliar Conference met in 1976, the issues of the "diaspora," autocephaly and autonomy were finally placed on the agenda for the projected Great and Holy Council, giving rise to further study of these subjects both on a popular and on a more scholarly level.[6] At long last, in

3 The letters in question, as well as other documents relating to the 1970 autocephaly, are available in English translation most conveniently in *St Vladimir's Theological Quarterly* 15 (1971), 42-80.

4 From the perspective of the OCA see the essay of Alexander Schmemann, "A Meaningful Storm: Some Reflections on Autocephaly, Tradition and Ecclesiology," *St Vladimir's Theological Quarterly* 15 (1971), 1-27, and also John Meyendorff, writing in *Contacts* no. 72 (1970). A very different perspective is taken by Panagiotes N. Trempelas, *The Autocephaly of the Metropolia in America* (Brookline, MA: Holy Cross Theological School Press, 1973).

5 "Meaningful Storm," 1.

6 In English on a popular level see, for example, Stanley S. Harakas, *Something Is Stirring in World Orthodoxy: An Introduction to the Forthcoming Great and Holy Council of the Orthodox Church* (Minneapolis: Light and

1990, the Interorthodox Preparatory Commission turned to the subject of the "diaspora" and adopted the first part of a text on that subject for submission to an eventual Fourth Pan-Orthodox Preconciliar Conference. In 1993 it adopted the second part of a text on the "diaspora" and a text on "autocephaly and how it is to be proclaimed," again for submission to an eventual Pan-Orthodox Preconciliar Conference. The draft text on the subject of autocephaly, like the text on the "diaspora," has not been officially released, since it has not yet been reviewed and approved by a Pan-Orthodox Preconciliar Conference. In addition, as the text itself indicates, further work is needed on at least one paragraph. But the French version of the text has been published by a leading consultant for the Secretariat for the Preparation of the Great and Holy Council.[7] It may not be wholly inappropriate, therefore, to offer an unofficial English translation at the present time:

Autocephaly and the Way in Which It Is To Be Proclaimed

The Interorthodox Preparatory Commission, after having labored on the basis of contributions from the most holy Orthodox churches and the report of the Secretary for the Preparation of the Great and Holy Council of the Orthodox

Life, 1978), esp. 19-31. Treatments of a more scholarly nature include John H. Erickson, "Autocephaly in Orthodox Canonical Literature to the Thirteenth Century," *St Vladimir's Theological Quarterly* 15 (1971), 28-41, revised and expanded in *The Challenge of Our Past* (Crestwood, NY: St Vladimir's Seminary Press, 1991), 91-113; Archbishop Pierre/Peter (L'Huillier), "Problems Concerning Autocephaly," *Greek Orthodox Theological Review* 24.2-3 (1979), 165-91 (part of an issue devoted to the Great and Holy Council), and "Accession to Autocephaly," *St Vladimir's Theological Quarterly* 37 (1993), 267-304.

7   Vlassios I. Phidas, *Droit Canon: Une Perspective Orthodoxe* (Chambésy/ Genève: Centre Orthodoxe du Patriarcat Oecuménique, 1998), 136-38.

Church on the question of *autocephaly and the way in which it is to be proclaimed,* examined the ecclesiological, canonical, pastoral and practical dimensions of the institution of autocephaly in the Orthodox Church and reached the following conclusions:

1. The institution of autocephaly expresses in an authentic way one of the fundamental aspects of the Orthodox ecclesiological tradition concerning relations between the local church and the universal Church of God. The profound connection between the canonical institution of ecclesiastical autocephaly and Orthodox ecclesiological teaching concerning the local church justifies the concern of the autocephalous local Orthodox churches for regulation of existing problems with regard to the correct functioning of the institution as much as it does their willingness to participate, through their detailed contributions, in the enhancement of the institution unto the advancement of the unity of the Orthodox Church.

2. The perichoresis between *locality* and *universality*, faithful to Orthodox ecclesiology, determines the functional relationship between administrative organization and the unity of the Church. Because of this, complete agreement was established with regard to the place of the institution of autocephaly in the life of the Orthodox Church.

3. Complete agreement was established concerning the canonical conditions which the proclamation of the autocephaly of a local church requires, namely the *consent* and action *of the mother church,* the *obtaining of a pan-Orthodox consensus,* and *the role of the Ecumenical Patriarchate* and the other autocephalous churches in the procedure of the proclamation of the autocephaly. According to the agreement:

a. The *mother church* which receives a request for autocephaly from an ecclesiastical region which depends on it evaluates whether the ecclesiological, canonical and pastoral conditions are satisfied for the granting of autocephaly. In the case where the local synod of the mother church, as its supreme ecclesiastical organ, gives its consent to the request, it submits the proposal on this subject to the Ecumenical Patriarchate so that pan-Orthodox consensus may be sought. The mother church informs the other local autocephalous churches of this.

b. According to pan-Orthodox practice, the Ecumenical Patriarchate communicates by patriarchal letter all the details concerning said request and seeks expression of pan-Orthodox consensus. Pan-Orthodox consensus is expressed by the unanimous decision of the synods of the autocephalous churches.

c. In expressing the consent of the mother church and the pan-Orthodox consensus, the Ecumenical Patriarch officially proclaims the autocephaly of the applying church by the publication of a patriarchal tomos. The tomos is signed by the Ecumenical Patriarch. It is desirable that it be co-signed by the primates of the autocephalous churches, but in any case it ought to be by the primate of the mother church.

Note: The content of paragraph 3c was referred for completion of scrutiny to the coming Interorthodox Preparatory Commission, which will seek out the consensus of the local churches on the question, thus completing its work on this theme.[8]

4. The local church proclaimed autocephalous is integrated into the communion of the autocephalous churches as a

8   Disagreement concerning the paragraph in question centered on whether the tomos of autocephaly should be issued by the mother church (the position of the Russian Orthodox Church and several others) or by the Patriarch of Constantinople (the position of that church and several others).

full-fledged member and enjoys all the canonical privileges hallowed by pan-Orthodox practice (diptychs, commemoration, interorthodox relations, etc.).

Notwithstanding the confident tone expressed in much of this text, full and definitive agreement on the subject of autocephaly still has not been reached. Even if agreement were reached concerning the substance and wording of paragraph 3c (and so far it has not been!), the text still remains simply a draft intended for submission to the Fourth Pan-Orthodox Preconciliar Conference. But that conference has not yet met, much less the Great and Holy Council to which the conference is supposed to submit its draft texts. In short, the storm of controversy prompted by the 1970 autocephaly of the OCA still has not ended. And in fact, pan-Orthodox agreement concerning autocephaly and related issues seems even more distant now than it was in 1970.

Why should this be? Certainly one reason is the complexity of the issues involved. It may be true that "The institution of autocephaly expresses in an authentic way one of the fundamental aspects of the Orthodox ecclesiological tradition concerning relations between the local church and the universal Church of God." But the history of this "institution" is much more complicated than our churches generally have been willing to acknowledge. During the controversy surrounding the 1970 autocephaly of the OCA, two clear-cut and seemingly mutually exclusive positions were put forward. Constantinople argued that only an ecumenical council can definitively establish an autocephalous church and that any interim arrangments depend upon approbation by Constantinople acting in its capacity as the "mother church" and "first among equals." The Russian Orthodox Church, on the other hand, argued that any autocephalous church has the right to grant canonical independence to one of its parts, provided that conditions necessary for independent church life are present (*e.g.,* an adequate number of bishops) and that this would be good and profitable for the ecclesiastical entity in question.[9] But neither the canons nor church history provides incontrovertible support for either one of these positions. Quite simply, as Professor Bogolepov's *Toward an American Orthodox Church* already indicated back in 1963, the Orthodox canonical tradition does not provide clear guidance on the subject of establishment of a new local church.

In a more recent and very thorough study of "Accession to Autocephaly," Archbishop Peter (L'Huillier) has pointed out this fact even more bluntly:

> We have shown that, beyond any doubt, historical evidence does not furnish a perennial procedural pattern which could be regarded as compelling, especially if we take into account the interference of factors which, through the ages, have partly distorted the original concept of autocephaly. Under such conditions, it would be difficult not to concur with this statement by the Ecumenical Patriarch Benjamin in 1937: "It is known... that concerning the manner in which the separation must occur and the manner of establishing the autocephaly of any part of the Church, none of the sacred canons provide direction or inkling."[10]

---

9   See the correspondence between the patriarchs of Moscow and Constantinople cited above, n. 3.

10 "Accession," 298, quoting the answer of Ecumenical Patriarch Benjamin to Patriarch Nicholas of Alexandria (December 7, 1937), in Apostolos Glavinas, *Orthodoxê Autocephalê Ekklêsia tês Albanias* (Thessalonica, 1985), 63.

But the absence of a "perennial procedural pattern" up until this point in the history of the Orthodox Church does not mean that the issue of autocephaly is insoluble or that confrontation and conflict over autocephaly are inevitable aspects of Orthodox church life. In the same article Archbishop Peter offers a very constructive observation:

> As has been evidenced by our historical survey, no canonical rule directly addressing this question has been enacted in the past, and precedents do not reveal an unquestionable model. Thus, it must be candidly acknowledged that this topic pertains to the sphere of the *de lege ferenda*. This implies that, within the parameters of the fundamental principles of our canonical Tradition, *a new law dealing with this specific question has to be promulgated.*[11]

Needed, in short, is new canonical activity along the lines set forth by the Interorthodox Preparatory Commission in its 1993 draft text, which would take into consideration the valid interests of the mother church, the need for pan-Orthodox consensus, and the importance of coordinating these various elements (the role of the Ecumenical Patriarchate). We can no longer afford simply to repeat old positions, particularly if these are based on questionable presuppositions or a distorted reading of church history. Now, more than ever, our churches need to demonstrate that our Orthodox canonical tradition is a living tradition, not just the sterile repetition of bygone formulas.

But pan-Orthodox agreement on the subject of autocephaly, whether through formal action of a Great and Holy Council or through less formal channels, is inconceivable in the absence a genuine spirit of trust among the

---

11 "Accession," 299, emphasis supplied.

churches. Through much of the twentieth century this spirit was noteworthy for its absence. Mutual fears of hegemonistic ambition led to one confrontation after another, and as the century drew to a close, tensions in inter-Orthodox relations were mounting rather than diminishing. Instead of bringing all the Orthodox churches closer together, the fall of communism in Russia and Eastern Europe in 1989-90 has brought to the surface many disagreements relating to church order that had been papered over during the previous decades. Here one needs only to mention the renewed conflict between the Russian Orthodox Church and the Patriarchate of Constantinople over the ecclesiastical status of Estonia (1995 onward). Even more ominous is the situation in Ukraine, where the Orthodox are now split among two self-proclaimed autocephalous churches and one autonomous church dependent on the Russian Orthodox Church. From our present vantage point, it is evident that the "storm" of controversy over the autocephaly of the OCA is simply part of a much larger weather system.

As developments over the last decade indicate, the problem of how a new local church is to be established still has not been resolved. Orthodoxy in America remains divided; a Great and Holy Council of the Orthodox Church still has not met; and the issues of autocephaly, autonomy and the "diaspora" are as divisive as ever. For this reason, Professor Bogolepov's *Toward an American Orthodox Church* remains timely and challenging. Some of the issues that he examines—for example, relations between the various "Russian" jurisdictions then competing for the faithful in America—now seem less pressing than they were before the collapse of communism in Russia and Eastern Europe. But the basic questions that Professor Bogolepov raises remain with us. What are the canonical requirements for establishing a new autocephalous church? What is the role of the mother church in establishing a new autocephalous church? What is the role of the ecumenical patriarch? What happens if a church proclaims its own independence? In approaching such questions, Professor Bogolepov—ever aware of the complex historical path of Orthodoxy—refuses to give one-sided or simplistic answers. His clear and sober presentation still merits careful reading and consideration.

John H. Erickson

INTRODUCTION

The establishment of a new autocephalous church is one of the basic problems of Orthodox Canon Law. The Ecumenical Councils of the fourth to eighth centuries recognized six independent churches: Rome, Constantinople, Alexandria, Antioch, Jerusalem, and Cyprus. After the separation of East and West, the five Eastern Churches remained in unity. The Florentine Union of 1439 led to the proclamation of the independence of the Russian Church from Constantinople (in 1448). With the disintegration of the Ottoman Empire, the Churches of Greece, Serbia, Romania, Bulgaria, and Albania also left the once great Church of Constantinople and became independent. After the First World War, more new Churches were founded, growing mainly out of the Russian Church. This is how the autocephalous Georgian, Polish, and Czechoslovak Churches came into being. As a result of all these changes, the total number of autocephalous Orthodox Churches had risen to 14 by the middle of the twentieth century. The unprecedented emigration following the First and Second World Wars resulted in the formation of new Orthodox church groups desiring their own administration independent of the Mother Church, which had the misfortune to fall under the control of Communist government. The situation became especially acute in America where parishes, missions, and dioceses of the autocephalous Orthodox Churches of Europe and Asia had been established since the latter part of the eighteenth century.

There has been an acute need, then, for regulation of the conditions and manner in which new autocephalous Orthodox Churches can, and should, be established. This problem was, and is, all the more complicated and difficult because the circumstances at the time of the founding of any new Church in the nineteenth and twentieth centuries have been radically different from those of the epoch of the first Ecumenical Councils, especially in countries of the New World, populated by immigrants under unprecedented political and religious conditions. The importance of achieving a proper solution of this problem was stressed by the 1961 Panorthodox Conference at Rhodes. This Conference gave a special place on the agenda of the forthcoming Pro-Synodal Conference to the prerequisites and conditions leading to the proclamation of autocephalous status, and also to the determination of the canonical status of the Orthodox Diaspora. The present work is an attempt to give a solution to this extremely important problem of the Orthodox Canon Law, based on canons and accepted Church practices, and thereby to establish criteria for the determination of the canonical status of the new ecclesiastical groups in America, under local conditions of religious freedom. At a time of increased contact among all Christians and the establishment of their mutual organizations, a clarification of this question may also promote a proper definition of the position of the Orthodox groups toward interdenominational bodies.

I

THE ESTABLISHMENT OF A NEW LOCAL CHURCH AS A PROBLEM OF ORTHODOX CANON LAW

The way in which new Orthodox Local Churches are established is of special significance for Orthodox Canon Law. As a legal problem, the establishment of a new Church is not significant, although for opposite reasons, either to Roman Catholicism or to Protestantism.

According to Roman Catholic teaching, the Church is one, not only because all its members profess the same faith and join in a common worship, but also because they are united by the guidance of the infallible successor of St. Peter, the Roman Pontiff. The unity of the Roman Catholic Church eliminates the possibility of any lawful separation from it. No new Church can be organized from a part of the Roman Church and legitimately become independent. From the Roman point of view, the true Christian Church can exist only under the authority of the Pope of Rome, the Visible Head of the Church and Christ's Vicar on Earth.

Unlike Roman Catholics, Protestants generally recognize the possibility of organizing new religious communities. Since preaching the Word of God is considered the basic task of the Church, each group of believers may, in its struggle for the right understanding of the Gospel, organize its own community with its own clergy. In Protestant practice, the establishment of a new body of clergy presents no canonical difficulties. It can even be established by the community itself. Since Protestantism recognizes the absolute supremacy of the Word, the Church is considered as founded on the teaching of Christ, that is "on Christ" but not "by Christ" and His Apostles.

In their struggle against the Roman Catholic Church, the Protestants (with some exceptions) rejected the idea of the uninterrupted succession of the spiritual authority from the Apostles. Since the appointment of pastors and ministers in most Protestant Churches is not connected with the reception of hierarchal authority from the successors of the Apostles, such appointment does not, therefore, depend on an existing hierarchy but rather depends solely on the community of believers. From the point of view of Protestant ecclesiology, nothing stands in the way of the separation of one or several communities from established Protestant Churches and the organization of new Protestant Churches. Complications may arise concerning the activities of ecclesiastical associations of citizens from civil authorities, but not from the Protestant concept of the Church. In spite of the successful collaboration of Protestant denominations in practical Christian work, Protestantism is not one Church but an aggregation of many Protestant Churches and communities which differ from one another both in their teachings and in their structures. In general the life of Protestantism is characterized by the establishment of ecclesiastical federations and associations.

The Orthodox Church retained the concept of Church unity which existed during the time of the seven Ecumenical Councils. (List and dates of these Councils will be found on page 130.) It is a unity in plurality of sister Churches, only some of which can have the privileges of honor. Its unity does not consist in the subordination to one single head. Orthodoxy recognizes no one to have been empowered by Christ to be His Vicar on earth and to have an indisputable authority above the whole of His Church. The deep spiritual unity of the sister Churches consists in the unity of faith, church tradition, basic features of canonical structure and divine services, as well as in the recognition of only that hierarchy which inherited its authority from the Apostles from all the Apostles, and not just from Peter. The Orthodox Church greatly values the connection of its hierarchy with the Apostles and, through them, with Christ Himself, and it firmly retains the principle of Apostolic Succession of hierarchal authority. With regard to the administration of internal affairs, the sister Churches enjoy equally the right of self-government and have independent ruling bodies. Administrative independence is provided for by differences in local usages but it is connected with a strong adherence to the basic principles of faith and Church order. The highest expressions of the Church's unity were the Ecumenical Councils.

Since the time of the Ecumenical Councils, the unity of the Church has been expressed in conferences of the heads of the Local Churches or of their representatives as well as in the correspondence of these heads in letters notifying others as to their accession to their sees, in reciprocal visits, in the exchanges of delegations, as well as in the acceptance of the decisions of the Highest Authorities of one or many Churches by other Local Churches, etc. Besides all this, the intercommunion in sacraments and worship has always been retained in full. Bishops and priests of one Local Church worship together with the bishops and priests of a sister Church; members of one Church partake in the sacraments and worship of other Churches. In this way the community of spiritual life and the unity of the whole Body of the Orthodox Church are secured, and an unrestricted subdivision of church structure as is found in the Protestant Churches is thereby eliminated.

The first four Ecumenical Councils not only recognized the principle that the Church consists of several administratively independent Local Churches but also established new Local Churches. In this way the possibility was created for establishing new Local Churches, whose number has never been limited.

This possibility, however, creates the problem of determining the canonical requirements for setting up such a new Local Church. This problem is more complicated for the Orthodox than it is for Protestants, because under Orthodox Canon Law the establishment of new Local Orthodox Churches is bound up with the fulfilling of certain requirements, such as securing the Apostolic Succession of hierarchal authority and maintaining unity among the sister Churches.

II

CANONICAL REQUIREMENTS FOR ESTABLISHING A NEW LOCAL CHURCH

The requirements for establishing new Local Churches are closely connected with peculiar features of their canonical position. The Orthodox sister Churches are autocephalous churches. We would search in vain for the word "autocephalous" (the Greek: "himself the head") in the canons adopted by the Ecumenical Councils. It was introduced by practice, and was used to denote a self-governing independent Church, a concept that had already been elaborated by the Ecumenical Councils.

Having recognized each of the five civil dioceses of the prefecture of the East as independent Churches, the Second Ecumenical Council (381) determined that the Bishops of Alexandria, Antioch, Asia (Minor), Pontus, and Thrace, may "alone administer the affairs" of their dioceses, without any interference from the bishops of other dioceses (Canon 2). Defending the independence of the Church of Carthage, the African Synod (424) also insisted in its letter to Pope Celestine, "That all matters should be terminated in the places where they arise." In addition, at the time that it recognized the independence of the Church of Cyprus from the Church of Antioch, the Third Ecumenical Council (431) declared that, "The Rulers of the holy churches in Cyprus shall enjoy, without dispute or injury... the right of performing for themselves the ordination of their excellent

Bishops" (Canon 8). Among the three bishops of Cyprus who presented their petition to the Third Ecumenical Council at Ephesus was the newly elected head of the Church of Cyprus, Bishop Rheginus. His election by the bishops of Cyprus was recognized as canonically valid. Therefore, there are two distinguishing marks of an autocephalous Church:

(1) The right to resolve all internal problems on its own authority, independently of all other Churches, and

(2) The right to appoint its own bishops, among them the head of the Church.

Besides autocephalous churches, there are also autonomous churches, and, in organization they differ substantially. The autocephalous church is a self-governing and administratively independent church, whereas the autonomous church has restricted self-government. Administratively, the latter depends upon an autocephalous church, under whose protection it stands. The distinguishing quality of an autonomous church is that it cannot have its own independent Head. Its Head can be elected by the local ecclesiastical bodies, but the election becomes valid only after it is confirmed by the Highest Authority of the autocephalous Church. The latter usually also has the right to supervise the activities of the autonomous church and to judge its bishops. Only an autocephalous church can be an immediate member of the community of Orthodox Sister Churches.

Accordingly, a part of the Orthodox Church claiming to be autocephalous must be sufficiently mature to organize its own ecclesiastical life; it must have a sufficient number of parishes and parishioners, the possibility of training new clergymen, and a hierarchy canonically capable of making subsequent appointments of new bishops. As to the last, canonically very important requirement, the canons distinguish between (a) the appointment of a bishop, that is, the designation of a person to hold the office of bishop, and (b) the ordination or consecration of the bishop. According to Canon 4 of the First Ecumenical Council, the appointment of a bishop can be made by "at least" three bishops of the Provincial Council of Bishops, and "then the ordination should take place." As to the consecration, it can be performed by as few as two bishops (Apostolic Canon 1); but it can take place only after the candidate has been appointed by the assembly of at least three ruling bishops, since the Provincial Council of Bishops consists only of bishops who administer dioceses belonging to the metropolitan district. If the number of ruling bishops of one Orthodox region is less than three, then this region cannot be proclaimed "autocephalous," since it is canonically unable to provide new bishops for itself.

Authority to appoint and consecrate a new bishop exists only when the three ruling bishops of an ecclesiastical region are themselves duly appointed and ordained, which means that they also had to be appointed and ordained by ruling bishops of one of the autocephalous Orthodox Churches having the "right of performing for themselves the ordination of their excellent Bishops" (Ephesian Canon 8). Since no autocephalous Church has the right to appoint bishops for any but its own dioceses, a bishop of a new Church originally had to be appointed by ruling bishops of one of the established autocephalous Churches to a diocese of that particular Church. As a result, the church region claiming autocephalous status must be a part of an autocephalous Church, its diocese, or its mission.

This rule has been deeply rooted in the practice of the Orthodox Church. Before proclaiming its independence in 1448, the Russian Church had been a metropolitan district of the Church of Constantinople. In the nineteenth and twentieth centuries, the Churches of Greece, Serbia, Romania, Bulgaria, and Albania were also dioceses of the Patriarchate of Constantinople before becoming independent. The Polish Orthodox Church was formed from dioceses of the Russian Church. The Church of Czechoslovakia included districts which had been under the jurisdiction of the Churches of Russia and Serbia, as well as some former Uniate dioceses which had come under the jurisdiction of Moscow. The autonomous Churches of Finland and China originated from parts of the Russian Church.

New Churches always originate in existing autocephalous Churches, and the whole Orthodox Church is like a tree which sends its branches in different directions; nevertheless, all the branches are fed by one sap and live one life. In this way the uninterrupted succession from the Apostles has really been preserved. Any ecclesiastical region which was not a part of an autocephalous Church may not claim to be autocephalous.

The presence of three canonically approved bishops and the canonical origin from one of the autocephalous Churches, however, give the right to claim an independent ecclesiastical administration only if the region is located in a state independent of that of its Mother Church. This requirement developed in the course of long Church practice, and derived from a system of establishing new Churches during the time of the Ecumenical Councils. For practical considerations, ecclesiastical districts were established from the very beginning of the Christian era in conformity with the political division of the state. Since, in the Roman Empire, the Christian Church became a state church, this practice was confirmed later by Canon 17 of the Council of Chalcedon (451), which stated: "Let the order of the ecclesiastical parishes follow the political and municipal pattern." The same regulation was renewed by Canon 38 of the Trullan Council (691), which reads: "...let the order of things ecclesiastical follow the civil and public models." Since the political division of the Roman Empire was based on the territorial principle, the same territorial principle was applied to the determination of the borders of ecclesiastical districts.

In the course of its development, the Roman Empire included in its boundaries some formerly independent states with populations consisting of different nationalities. Consequently, its political land administrative division reflected, to a certain extent, the national characteristics of the countries absorbed. National peculiarities of the different regions were much more preserved in the lower administrative districts than in the higher ones, but the territorial principle was paramount.

Following the civil and public models, the administrative division of the Church also reflected, to some extent, the national composition of the Roman Empire, though here too the territorial principle predominated.

Apostolic Canon 34 mentions the national principle in the lower church districts; according to this canon, "The bishops of every nation (*ethnos*), must acknowledge him who is first among them. The language of this canon has been cited to support the contention that the nation should be the basis of Church organization. However, the Council of Antioch (341) gave the most authoritative interpretation to the word "nation" (*ethnos*); its Canon 9 explains "nation" (*ethnos*), not as meaning a people bound together by ties of blood, language, and customs, but as meaning a "province"—the administrative subdivision of the civil diocese of the Roman Empire. This Canon 9 of Antioch, which in effect reproduces the 34th Apostolic Canon, reads: "It behoves the bishops in every province [in Greek-*eparchia*] to acknowledge the bishop who presides in the metropolis..." Thus, in the middle of the fourth century the territorial principle was recognized as paramount for the establishment and government of ecclesiastical districts, regardless of whether or not they conformed to the national principle. The national principle was significant only so far as it coincided with the territorial principle, but it did not override it.

Later in the history of Orthodox Canon Law, this correlation of the territorial and the national principles was interpreted to mean that a new autocephalous Church could only be established for a nation lying within the borders of a state independent of that of the Mother Church. From the tenth century, this point of view was accepted by the new Balkan nations: Bulgaria, Serbia, and Romania, which had all received Christianity from Constantinople. The Church in these states had the same character as that of Byzantium, that is, a state-church. After these nations had acquired their independence, efforts were made to withdraw their Churches from subordination to Constantinople and to establish them as independent church administrations. Many years later, the Russian Church did the same.

In the *Kormchaya Kniga* (The Rudder) published by Patriarch Nikon in 1653, the establishment of these new Churches, as well as the secession of the Russian Church from the Patriarchate of Constantinople, was justified. In the introductory chapters of the *Kormchaya Kniga* it was explained that the fact of having received Christianity from Constantinople did not mean that the Church must be subordinated to the Patriarch of Constantinople forever. The argument said further that if a nation has established an independent state not subordinate to the Greek Empire, and if the Local Church gradually becomes stronger, it also may in time become self-governing and independent. The initiative can be taken, as was the case with the Bulgarian Church, by the Tsar, who very "justly" decided to appoint a Patriarch nominated by the Bulgarian Bishops' Sobor in Trnovo. It is also possible to obtain the necessary consent of the Greek Emperor and the Patriarch of Constantinople, as occurred in Serbia, where the Patriarch was appointed by the local bishops. As for Russia, the *Kormchaya Kniga* stressed the extreme significance of the Russian Principality since ancient times and the high authority of the Russian Tsar, describing the sublimity of the state of Moscow and the growth of its piety. It was pointed out as a strange inconsistency that the Russian metropolitans were still appointed by the Patriarch of Constantinople and that, despite the long distance, they had to go to Constantinople for their appointment. The submission of all the Eastern Churches to the Moslem Turkish rule was mentioned as a further obstacle to the Russian metropolitans going to Constantinople (pp. 5-10). By all this the idea was emphasized that an independent Orthodox Church can be established in an independent state.[1]

The above principle was generally recognized at the Synod of 1593 in Constantinople, even by the Patriarchal See of Constantinople. The question was raised at that Synod whether canonical rules allowed the establishment of a Patriarchal See in Moscow, and whether the Russian Church could be recognized as autocephalous. An affirmative answer to this question was obtained through the interpretation of Canon 28 of Chalcedon, according to which the Patriarchal See of Constantinople had received its privileges because Constantinople was a Royal City, honored with the Sovereignty and the Senate. The same argument was applied to the See of Moscow, which could also be recognized as worthy of the Patriarchal dignity, since Moscow was a Royal City of the Russian Kingdom.[2]

The principle, "An autocephalous Church in an independent state," was later approved and developed in detail by the Ecumenical Patriarch, Joachim III, in his letter concerning the recognition of the Serbian Church in 1879. This Letter is an answer to the letters of the Serbian Prince Milan Obrenovich and Michael, the Metropolitan of Belgrade, requesting that the Serbian Church be granted independence. After having given careful consideration to this problem, Patriarch Joachim III, together with his Holy Synod, recognized that self-governing Local Churches may be established "not only in conformity with the historical importance of the cities and countries in Christianity, but also according to political conditions of the life of their people and nations." Referring then to Canon 28 of Chalcedon and to other canons, as well as to the opinion of Patriarch Photius, Patriarch Joachim III reaffirmed: "The ecclesiastical rights, especially those of parishes, usually conform to the structure of the state authority and its provinces." The Letter goes on, "Whereas, the pious and God-protected principality of Serbia has, through God's Providence, gained strength, has increased, and has attained complete political independence; and, Whereas, the most pious Prince Milan M. Obrenovich IV and His Eminence, Michael, Archbishop of Belgrade and Metropolitan of Serbia, on behalf of the honorable clergy and pious people, requested us by letter to grant autocephalous and independent ecclesiastical status…" the Patriarch and the Holy Synod found that "the request was well grounded and conformed to the spirit of Sacred canons and to the Church practice," and therefore decided "to proclaim the Holy Serbian Church autocephalous, independent and self-governing."[3]

This decision is of extreme importance because the granting of autocephalous status is conditioned directly upon the location of the Church in a politically independent state, so that the foundation of a new Church under such circumstances is recognized as being "in conformity to the spirit of the Sacred canons and to Church practice." The same idea was used by the Ecumenical Patriarch Gregory VII as a basis of his Patriarchal and Synodal Canonical Tomos of November 13, 1924, giving the reasons for granting the autocephalous status to the Orthodox Church in the reestablished Polish state. When referring to Canon 17 of the Fourth Ecumenical Council and Canon 36 of the Trullan Council, Patriarch Gregory VII states that the structure of ecclesiastical affairs has to follow the political and public forms. Therefore, a Church district of canonical origin having no less than three duly appointed ruling bishops may receive autocephalous status if it be situated in a politically independent state.

It is true that the Letter of Patriarch Joachim III concerned the Serbian Church as a national one, but even in this case the national principle was again subordinated to the territorial; the Serbian Church was recognized as independent, as long as its members were within the borders of the state of Serbia. However, the Orthodox Serbs living outside the Serbian state, for example in Austria, were not regarded as belonging to the autocephalous Serbian Church, and they were not granted its privileges. On the other hand, the political-territorial principle cannot prevent members of one nationality group, within the borders of an independent Church, from living side by side with members of another ethnic group as citizens of the same state. In multinational states, the political-territorial principle comes close to the concept of a "nation-state," which includes all citizens of that state, regardless of their nationality.

Later, the independence of a state as a prerequisite for obtaining autocephalous status for the Church was also stressed by Patriarch Alexis at the Moscow Conference of 1948. Actually, Patriarch Alexis only repeated the reasons mentioned in the *Kormchaya Kniga* by Patriarch Nikon, but at the same time he defined them more exactly and gave some additional reasons. His most important points were:

(1) The number of bishops in the Russian Church far exceeded the minimum canonically required for the establishment of an independent Church.

(2) The Russian Church found herself within another state which possessed an enormous territory and was quite independent of the state in which her Mother Church of Constantinople was located.

(3) Her faithful belonged to another nation, which had a different language, different habits, and different customs.

(4) It became more and more obvious that there was a need not only for having a Russian Metropolitan as head of the Russian Church but also for having the right of appointing him independently of the Patriarch of Constantinople by a Council of Russian Bishops.

In addition, Patriarch Alexis mentioned the great distance between Constantinople and Moscow (just as Patriarch Nikon did in the *Kormchaya Kniga*), the instability of the Greek Church in Orthodoxy, the fall of Constantinople into the bands of the Turks (which threatened the Church with the loss of the purity of its faith), and the fact that the Bulgarian and Serbian Churches had long since received autocephalous status, although they were smaller than the Russian Church and were situated nearer to Constantinople.

The complete list of the prerequisites for establishing a new Local Church given by Patriarch Alexis is important because the Patriarch indicated some additional conditions which might justify separation from a Mother Church.

Patriarch Alexis mentioned the instability of the Greek Church in Orthodoxy. He asserted that the Russian Church could preserve the Orthodox faith pure and intact only by becoming completely independent of the Church of Constantinople.[4] This statement by Patriarch Alexis evidently rested upon Canons 13-15 of the First-and-Second Council of 861 in Constantinople. These canons permit and even approve withdrawing from communion with higher ecclesiastical authorities who publicly preach a heresy already condemned by the Holy Councils or Fathers.

Since the hierarchy of the Russian Church of the present has been compelled to support the Communist government in both internal and external difficulties in return for permission to reestablish the shattered hierarchical structure of the Church and for some freedom of performing divine services, the Russian hierarchy usually asserts that secession from the Russian Church would be lawful only if they should openly preach heresy (Letter of Patriarchal Locum Tenens, Metropolitan Sergius, December 31, 1927).[5]

The attempt to limit the reasons for separation to dogmatic problems or to treat canonical reasons as dogmatic is unjustified. The provisions concerning reasons for secession are not limited to Canons 13-15 of the First-and-Second Council in 861. They are also found in Apostolic Canon 31, which forbade the secession of a presbyter from his bishop, if the presbyter did so without first condemning his bishop before the Bishops' Council for doing something wrong not only with regard to "piety" but also with regard to "righteousness." The public preaching of heresy can be understood as an infringement of piety, while the violation of righteousness includes violations of ecclesiastical order and of the rules of organization and administration of the Church. The validity of the Apostolic Canons, recognized by the Trullan and the Seventh Ecumenical Councils, is higher than that of the canons of the First-and-Second Council of 861 which was a Local Council, whose canons

do not belong to the general Canonical Code of the Orthodox Church as established by the Ecumenical Councils.
Therefore, Canons 13-15 of the Council of 861 are no restric-
tion on the broader meaning of the 31st Apostolic Canon and,
hence, the reasons for secession can be canonical as well as
dogmatic.

Patriarch Alexis also regarded the subordination of
Constantinople to the Moslem yoke as a danger to the purity
of the Orthodox faith, though this subordination could not
have been the immediate reason for the separation of the
Russian Church from the Patriarchate of Constantinople.
The Greek Metropolitan of Moscow, Isidore, was deposed in
Moscow in 1441; and in 1448 a new Russian Metropolitan,
Jonah, was elected in his place by the Russian Sobor. Thus
the Russian Church had become independent of the Church
of Constantinople before that city's seizure by the Turks in
1453. But the Moslem yoke could still have been the reason
for Moscow's maintaining its independence which had been
proclaimed earlier. The Russian apprehensiveness about
injury to Orthodoxy in Constantinople under the Turks was,
of course, exaggerated. However, the Russian Church faced
the real danger that its head might become dependent on the
Moslem Sultan if Russian metropolitans were still appointed in Constantinople. Like all appointments of bishops
made by the Ecumenical Patriarch, the appointment of the
Metropolitan for Moscow would have had to be approved
by the Sultan. The Russian candidates would have been
obliged to make a long trip to Constantinople, visit the
Sultan, and make to him the necessary payments in order to
receive confirmation of their right to the Moscow See.[6] The
dependence of the Ecumenical Patriarch upon the Sultan

could have impaired the free development of ecclesiastical life in the Russian State. Patriarch Alexis rightly emphasized the dependence of the Mother Church on a non-Christian power as one of the reasons for the establishment of an independent ecclesiastical administration.

If an ecclesiastical region not only fulfills the three principal requirements necessary for receiving autocephalous status (canonical origin, presence of at least three duly appointed bishops, and location in a state other than that of the Mother Church), but also has other reasons forcing it to separate from its Mother Church, then these additional reasons take on special importance; they force the ecclesiastical region to use its canonical rights to complete independence and speed up the process of separation from the Mother Church.

It must also be noted that Patriarch Alexis took a strong legal stand. He gave a full account of the reasons for ecclesiastical independence in order to prove that the "Russian Church even in the first years of its existence had a right to more than it had received in the field of its Church administration," by which he meant that it should have had a more independent administration than that which it had. In his conclusion Patriarch Alexis emphasized that the Russian Church "possessed all the canonical prerequisites not only for autonomous, but also for autocephalous status."[7]

If a Church meets all the canonical requirements for autocephalous status, then justice requires that its claim be recognized and that it be included in the number of autocephalous Churches. "Rights" always correspond with "duties" of others to act according to these rights.

III

THE RECOGNITION OF A NEW LOCAL CHURCH AT THE TIME OF THE ECUMENICAL COUNCILS

The recognition of autocephalous status is the final act in the establishment of a new and independent Church. From that moment on, it becomes a full and equal member of the community of autocephalous Churches of the Orthodox Church. The introduction of a new member into this community is of common concern to all its members. Therefore, such an innovation can occur only with the consent of all the other autocephalous Churches.

During the time of the Ecumenical Councils all new independent Churches were recognized, or established, by Ecumenical Councils themselves. The independence of the Churches of Rome, Alexandria, and Antioch was recognized by the First Ecumenical Council. The Churches of Thrace, Asia Minor, and Pontus were proclaimed independent by the Second Ecumenical Council. The independence of the Church of Cyprus was established by the Third Ecumenical Council. The Fourth Ecumenical Council subordinated the Churches of Thrace, Asia Minor, and Pontus to the authority of the Archbishop of Constantinople and at the same time founded the Church of Constantinople; the same Council also proclaimed the Church of Jerusalem to be independent.

When the Ecumenical Councils ceased to convene, Church practice from the tenth to the twentieth centuries knew two methods by which the existence of new Churches was officially recognized: (1) by the Mother Church, and (2) by the Ecumenical Patriarch. Under either method, the other autocephalous Churches joined in the recognition.

IV

THE RECOGNITION OF A NEW CHURCH
BY THE MOTHER CHURCH

The prerogative of the Mother Church to recognize a new Church was strongly defended in a letter by Alexis, Patriarch of Moscow, to the Ecumenical Patriarch, Athenagoras (March 7, 1953). "Until rules have been established by which one part of a Local Church may be proclaimed autocephalous," this letter states, "legal force shall be attributed to the practice of establishing an autocephalous church by the decision of the Council of Bishops of its Mother Church, which alone has the right to decide on matters such as the granting of autocephalous, as well as autonomous, status to one of its parts. Of this fact numerous examples can be provided."[8]

As appears from this letter, "rules" for proclaiming one part of a Local Church autocephalous or autonomous have not yet been established and hence the rights of the Mother Church are based upon the existing order, relying on "numerous examples" taken from Church practice or Church customs. But Church practices can have special legal force only if they conform to canons. In order to prove the privilege of the Mother Church to establish new Local Churches, reference is usually made to Apostolic Canon 31 as well as Canons 13, 14, and 15 of the First and Second Council (see letter of the Patriarchal Locum Tenens, Metropolitan Sergius, of January 5, 1935, to Archbishop Benjamin, Patriarchal Exarch in America). But none of these canons is concerned with establishing a new Local Church.

Apostolic Canon 31 prescribes that a presbyter be deposed who despises his own bishop, collects a separate congregation, and erects another altar without having any grounds for condemning his bishop with regard to piety or righteousness. Canon 13 of the First-and-Second Council also provides that any presbyter or deacon shall be subject to deposition if he, on the ground that his own bishop has been condemned for certain crimes, should dare to secede from his communion before the Council of Bishops has examined the charges. The same sanction was laid down in Canon 14 for a bishop who withdraws from communion with his metropolitan, and in Canon 15, for any presbyter, bishop, or metropolitan who breaks away from his patriarch. All these canons of the Council of 861 forbid the arbitrary withdrawal of clergymen from communion with their higher ecclesiastical authorities (except when the bishop publicly preaches a heresy which has already been condemned by the Holy Councils).

(1) These canons mention only personal acts of individual clergymen—the withdrawal by a deacon or presbyter from communion with his bishop, by the bishop from communion with his metropolitan, or by a metropolitan, bishops, or presbyters from communion with their patriarch, regardless of whether the flock joins them. Even if a part of the flock follows them, the withdrawn part is canonically unable to continue an independent Church life. By contrast, whenever a new Church is established, it is not one presbyter, or one bishop, or one metropolitan who withdraws from

Church communion, but rather an entire region; and its population, clergy, and no less than three bishops withdraw not from communion but only from administrative dependence.

(2) The Council of 861 considered the withdrawal of a bishop or metropolitan from communion with his patriarch on a level with that of a presbyter from his bishop or patriarch. It is very clear that the Council of 861 was concerned only with internal strife (the secession of the adherents of Ignatius from Patriarch Photius) and did not provide regulations for the separation of a part of the Church situated in a country completely independent from Byzantium. Whereas, the founding of a new autocephalous Church depends upon the location of the Church in a region within the boundaries of a state other than that of its Mother Church.

(3) Apostolic Canon 31 and Canons 13-15 of the First-and-Second Council deal only with splits which occur as a result of charges brought forward against certain hierarchs. When the withdrawal occurs before these charges are heard by the Council of Bishops, it is looked upon as a schism—an illicit, arbitrary split—and those found guilty are subject to ecclesiastical sanctions: deposition or excommunication. But the establishing of a new Church may occur without any charges against the hierarchy of the Mother Church, and may be simply on the grounds that this region has reached maturity for self-government and has fulfilled all canonical requirements necessary for the foundation of a new Church.

All of the foregoing only proves that Apostolic Canon 31 and Canons 13-15 of the First-and-Second Council have no importance in the problem of establishing a new Church, especially since that problem first arose at a later date. Hence, the claim of the privilege of the Mother Church to grant autocephalous status to one of its parts cannot be based on these canons. Although single presbyters and deacons cannot withdraw without the consent of their higher ecclesiastical authorities, that is no ground for concluding that the establishing of a new Local Church is likewise possible only with the consent of the head of the Mother Church and its Council of Bishops. The canons and practices of the Orthodox Church clearly distinguish between the withdrawal of a presbyter, bishop, or metropolitan from the jurisdiction of higher Church authorities and the establishment of a new Local Church.

The distinction between the separation of clergymen from communion with their superiors and the establishing of a new Local Church is of great importance for the understanding of the canonical meaning of different types of separation in the Orthodox Church. While the withdrawal of clergymen from communion with their hierarchal superiors is generally an illicit and arbitrary action, the establishing of a new Local Church is not necessarily a schism but may be canonically lawful. Consequently, persons taking part in the canonical organization of a new Church are not liable to punishment, as required by the First and Second Council of 861.

The opinion that the Mother Church alone is entitled to grant autocephalous status not only has no basis in the canons reviewed, but is also inconsistent with the principles of Orthodox Canon Law. If the Council of Bishops of the Mother Church "alone" has the right to grant autocephalous status to a part of its Church, then, necessarily, no other autocephalous Church has any voice in this matter. Presumably, if the Council of Bishops of the Mother Church does not recognize the autocephalous status of the new Church, the other Churches have no authority to do so; likewise, according to the letter of Patriarch Alexis of Moscow, after autocephalous status has been granted by the Mother Church, all the Sister Churches must enter into canonical communion with that Church, thus acknowledging the legality of the founding of the new Church by the will of the Mother Church.

In the same letter, the Patriarch of Moscow expressed his bewilderment as to why, "contrary to the canons and tradition of the Church," the Ecumenical Patriarch did not enter into canonical communion with the Polish and Czechoslovakian Churches, "despite the fact that their autocephalous status has been recognized by the Moscow Patriarchate as their Mother Church." Evidently, according to the letter of Patriarch Alexis, the Sister Churches must recognize the autocephalous status granted by the Mother Church. Thus, a change which ought to be decided by the whole community of autocephalous Local Churches becomes an internal problem of one of the autocephalous Churches, and the latter confers upon itself a right which belongs to the entire community of Local Churches.

Such an interpretation of the right of the Mother Church does not conform to the canonical principles of the Ecumenical Councils. The recognition of the autocephalous status of one of its parts by the Mother Church cannot deprive the Sister Churches of their independent right to pass on the legality of such a move. One member of the community of Orthodox Churches cannot, by itself, introduce a new Church into the community without the consent of all the other members, who are equal in status. The Patriarchal See in Constantinople, just as every other autocephalous Church, has the right to withhold recognition of the autocephalous status of a new Church, as granted by its Mother Church. Therefore, the refusal of the Ecumenical Patriarch to enter into canonical communion with the heads of the Polish and Czechoslovakian Churches cannot be considered as an act "contrary to the canons and traditions of the Church," as claimed in the letter of the Patriarch of Moscow. By declining to recognize the autocephalous status of these Churches, the Ecumenical Patriarch was exercising the basic right of every autocephalous Church, and especially of the first among them.

The separation of a new Church from an existing autocephalous Church is usually a rather painful procedure: even for a Church covering a large region, it is hard to lose one of its parts. In this connection, it is especially useful for the Mother Church to seek the opinions of its Sister Churches, which may differ from its own.

The Third Ecumenical Council in 341 recognized the Church of Cyprus as independent of the Church of Antioch, despite the claim of the Bishop of Antioch to ordain bishops for Cyprus as officers of the Antiochian Church. The life of the entire Orthodox Church is based on the intercommunion of all Local Churches, each of which has the right to decide independently on the eligibility of one of the parts of an autocephalous Church to be self-governing.

V

THE RECOGNITION OF A NEW CHURCH BY THE ECUMENICAL PATRIARCH

The system of recognition of a new Church by the Ecumenical Patriarch did not precede the system of recognition by the Mother Church. From the tenth to the twentieth centuries both procedures were used together.

The Patriarchate of Constantinople was also a Mother Church from which new Churches separated. Their recognition by the head of their Mother Church constituted recognition by the Ecumenical Patriarch, so autocephalous status was granted by the act of the one Church only, that is, by the decision of the Patriarch of Constantinople and his Synod of Bishops. Contrary to the practice at the time of the Ecumenical Councils, the ancient Patriarchates of Alexandria, Antioch, and Jerusalem thereafter did not enjoy the same rights as the Church of Constantinople. Especially during the Turkish domination from the fifteenth to the nineteenth centuries, the representatives of those Patriarchates were unable to resist the authority of the Patriarch of Constantinople.

An example of this inequality is the procedure by which the Patriarchate of Moscow was recognized. The Ecumenical Patriarch Jeremias II made that decision alone. When visiting Moscow in 1589 he recognized the Patriarchal dignity of the See of Moscow and attended the enthronement of the newly appointed Russian Patriarch. Only later, in

1590 and then in 1593, were synods convoked in Constantinople to discuss the Russian question, partly upon the insistence of the Russian Government. The sessions of the Synod in 1590 were attended by Joachim, the Patriarch of Antioch, and Sophronios, the Patriarch of Jerusalem. (Sylvester, the Patriarch of Alexandria, died shortly before the sessions.) That Synod confirmed the personal decision of Patriarch Jeremias II. At the same time the Patriarchs of Antioch and Jerusalem publicly acknowledged their dependence upon the Patriarch of Constantinople. By the Synodal decision the duty was imposed upon the new Patriarch of Moscow "to respect the Apostolic See of Constantinople as Head and Authority...just as the other Patriarchs respect him." The new Patriarch of Alexandria, Meletios Pegas, was displeased by this decision and sent Patriarch Jeremias a letter in which he wrote: "I know for certain that you were wrong to elevate the Moscow Metropolitanate to a Patriarchate because...the right to decide on this matter belongs not to the Patriarch alone but to the Synod and even to the Ecumenical Synod (Council). Therefore," Patriarch Meletios continued, "Your Holiness should obtain the consent of the other brethren... Since our words do not lead You to any thing good, but only bring You confusion, anger, and their consequences, I relieve Your Holiness from my reproaches and myself from trouble." Later on, at the Synod sessions in 1593, Patriarch Meletios himself supported the previous decision of 1590 on the establishment of the Patriarchate of Moscow.[9]

In the nineteenth century, autocephalous status was granted to the Churches of Greece (1850), Serbia (1879), and Romania (1885) by means of synodal tomos (decrees) of the Ecumenical Patriarch.

What was the Ecumenical Patriarch's basis for exercising such extensive powers? No such basis could be expected in the canons of the Seven Ecumenical Councils; even the title "Ecumenical" is not to be found in them. This title, first used in letters of Byzantine Emperors, was canonically conferred upon the Patriarch of Constantinople in 586 by the Synod of the See of Constantinople, that is, by the local law of the Church of Constantinople itself. Nevertheless, the title "Ecumenical" was eventually accepted by all other Orthodox Churches. Its significance had to be established by Church practices and customs and to this day has not been completely accepted.

Although the history of the Patriarchate of Constantinople is full of tragic events, the powers of the Patriarch himself were broadened by both the Byzantine Emperors and, later, the Turkish Sultans. His authority with regard to other Churches increased. The Byzantine Emperors made the Patriarch of Constantinople an intermediary between themselves and other patriarchs and bishops. The Patriarchs of Alexandria, Antioch, and Jerusalem might be granted an audience with the Emperor only upon the recommendation of the Patriarch of Constantinople and, as a result, they became dependent upon him. Later, the Turkish Sultan proclaimed the Patriarch of Constantinople the Head and Ruler of all Christians in the Ottoman Empire. The ancient Patriarchs of Alexandria, Antioch, and Jerusalem were usually appointed by the Sultan upon the recommendation of the Patriarch of Constantinople and became dependent upon him even more than they were at the time of the Byzantine Empire.

The Eastern Patriarchates, Alexandria, Antioch and Jerusalem, fell under the control of Constantinople more easily because they had become extremely weak following the loss of some of their dioceses as a result of dogmatic controversies. In fact, they were nearly destroyed by the invasion of the Arabs and by the Crusaders, and only with the subsequent help of the Patriarch of Constantinople was the life of their Churches restored. Sometimes the ancient patriarchal sees could not be filled and a titular Patriarch, appointed by the Ecumenical Patriarch, resided in Constantinople. Together with the ancient Patriarchates, the formerly independent Churches of Bulgaria and Serbia also came under the jurisdiction of the Ecumenical Patriarch, in consequence of the subordination of their countries to the Turks.

Thus, within the boundaries of the Turkish Empire, a large multinational Orthodox Church was formed, headed by the Ecumenical Patriarch, who used not only the honorific prerogatives established by the Ecumenical Councils (Second Ecumenical Council, Canon 3; Fourth Ecumenical Council, Canon 28) but also jurisdictional powers whose basis lay outside the canons.

When, in the nineteenth century, the National Churches of Greece, Serbia, Bulgaria, and Romania, one after another, began to secede from the Church of Constantinople, the Ecumenical Patriarch alone decided on their canonical status. The establishing of a new Church meant withdrawal from the jurisdiction of the Ecumenical Patriarch. Under such conditions, it became accepted that a new Church could be established with the consent only of the Ecumenical Patriarch and his Synod, and that its independence might be recognized by him alone. Only the Russian Church was completely independent from Constantinople, but it too had seceded from the Ecumenical Patriarch and regarded all new secessions as internal affairs of the Church of Constantinople.

Evidently it was to this practice of the Church of Constantinople that Patriarch Alexis of Moscow referred in his letter of March 7, 1953 (see page 23). The canonical validity of that reference can be evaluated only after a judgment is reached on the problem of whether this Church practice, which arose under peculiar political conditions, can serve as a general rule for all future periods.

A Church practice cannot take on binding force simply because it has been followed for a long time. To become a Church custom, a practice must be (a) in conformity to the basic principles of faith and Church order, and (b) repeated freely. The binding force of a custom derives from that Church consciousness which accepts a certain line of action as correct. Church consciousness can, of course, be evidenced in any action performed freely, without the use of force. The practice of establishing new Churches solely with the consent of the Patriarch of Constantinople was created on the basis of his powers obtained from the Byzantine Emperors and the Turkish Sultans. But the acts of state power are measures of compulsion, and a Church practice based upon acts of state fails to attain the standing of a Church custom for lack of one of the most important conditions—the freedom of formation. Sometimes the Church has no choice but to follow some laws and orders of the state, but civil laws can never be considered sources of Canon Law, which is created by the Church itself.

Similarly, the recognition of the prerogatives of the Ecumenical Patriarch by other Local Churches of the Ottoman Empire cannot support the canonical validity of such prerogatives, since those prerogatives were derived from the decrees of the Ottoman Empire, and the other Churches were compelled to comply with those decrees. No recognition imposed by the state can be canonically valid, any more than acquiescence by the Church of Constantinople in arbitrary appointments and depositions of patriarchs and bishops by Byzantine Emperors and Turkish Sultans could bring about any alteration of the canonical procedure for their appointments and depositions. Afterwards, when the other ancient patriarchates had an opportunity to use the same Sultan's authority to loosen their dependence upon the Patriarch of Constantinople, they succeeded in reestablishing the right of their bishops to elect their own Patriarch: Jerusalem in 1845, Antioch and Alexandria in 1899. The other Churches separated themselves from the Church of Constantinople at the time of the disintegration of the Ottoman Empire and gradually became independent of the Ecumenical Patriarch.

The concept that recognition of a new Church is the exclusive privilege of the Ecumenical Patriarch, or that his approval must precede any subsequent recognition by other Local Churches, is as inconsistent with the principles of Orthodox Canon Law as the equally misunderstood right of the Mother Church discussed above. In both cases, the error would allow one Local Church to decide an interorthodox question, and the rights of that Church are put above the rights of all the Sister Churches.

It must be admitted that, after the Ecumenical Patriarch became Head and Ruler of all Christians in the Turkish Empire, and when the establishment of a new Church necessarily meant withdrawal from his jurisdiction, the recognition of new Local Churches by him was the only possible procedure. But under new conditions, when the number of autocephalous Churches has increased considerably, that system cannot stand, since it is inconsistent with the canonical principles and practices of the times of the Ecumenical Councils. The Moscow Patriarch's attempt to base the right of the Mother Church to establish an autocephalous Church upon that practice of the Church of Constantinople which arose under particular historic conditions lacks sufficient foundation.

VI

THE RECOGNITION OF NEW CHURCHES SINCE THE BEGINNING OF THE TWENTIETH CENTURY

The theory of the exclusive right of a Mother Church to grant autocephalous status, so insistently defended by Patriarch Alexis, can be regarded as nothing but the transfer of the prerogatives of the Church of Constantinople to the new Russian Mother Church. It is easy to understand that these two principles had to collide, as they actually did after the First World War. At this time the insufficiencies of both principles were revealed and, at the same time, fresh approaches to the problem of recognizing new autocephalous Churches came to light.

From the middle of the fifteenth century to the beginning of the nineteenth century the life of the Orthodox Church proceeded in such a manner that not only did the Ecumenical Council cease to convene but even contact among the autocephalous Churches, based upon mutual equality, was lost. During this period the concept of the Orthodox Church as a unity in plurality, as a community of equal autocephalous Churches with only prerogatives of honor among them, disappeared. This community could not exist so long as there were only two truly independent Local Churches: the Church of Constantinople and the Russian Church. In fact the synodal structure of the latter suffered in comparison with the old Patriarchal dignity of the Church of Constantinople.

The reestablishment of the community of Orthodox Local Churches became possible only after the reestablishment of the independence of the ancient Eastern Patriarchates and other Churches which, during the period of Turkish rule, had become dependent upon Constantinople. Several wars of liberation of the nineteenth century in which Russia took an active part freed Greece, Serbia, Romania, and Bulgaria from Turkish rule and, as a result, they started to organize their own independent Churches. In spite of the protests of the Patriarch of Constantinople, the Russian Imperial Government supported before the Sublime Portc (Turkish Government) the requests of the ancient Patriarchates to elect their own candidates for the Patriarchal Sees in Jerusalem (1845), Damascus (1899), and Alexandria (1899). The reestablishment of the independence of these Churches was made possible through the influence of the Russian Church, whose voice could more readily be heard since it was a state Church and coincided with the political interests of the Russian Government. As a result of the disintegration of the Turkish Empire, the community of free Orthodox Churches was organized anew. By the beginning of the twentieth century there were ten Local Churches: Constantinople, Alexandria, Antioch, Jerusalem, Cyprus, Russia, Greece, Serbia, Romania, and Bulgaria. These Local Churches undertook to display their own will, and the importance of the Ecumenical Patriarch in the matter of the recognition of new Churches gradually ebbed.

A dispute with the Patriarch of Constantinople had become apparent for the first time after the latter refused to recognize the Bulgarian Exarchate established by the Imperial Decree (Firman) of the Turkish Government in 1870. In

1872 the Patriarch of Constantinople invited representatives of the Churches of Russia and Serbia, together with the Patriarchs of the ancient Eastern Churches to a council in Constantinople to censure the Bulgarian Church for this action. However, the Russian Holy Synod refused to participate in this council, claiming that the dispute was purely an internal affair of the Church of Constantinople. The Serbian Church also refused to participate. Later, the Russian Church did not associate itself with the decision of this council. It also avoided common celebration of the Divine Liturgy with Bulgarian clergymen for a long time, though members of the Bulgarian Church were always admitted to communion and other sacraments in Russian churches and vice versa. In this case, the right of the Mother Church of Constantinople to grant autocephalous status was not questioned but concurrence in a censure of the Bulgarian Church was withheld.

A very clear case of nonrecognition of the acts of the Ecumenical Patriarchal See in Constantinople occurred soon after the First World War. The Ecumenical Patriarch recognized the establishment of new Churches in the republics of Estonia, Latvia, Finland, and Poland, which had separated from the Russian Church. In this case there was a differentiation between the functions of the Archbishop of Constantinople as Head of the Mother Church and as Ecumenical Patriarch; it seems clear that here he acted only as the Ecumenical Patriarch. "Since the Most Holy Apostolic Patriarchal See in Constantinople" considered it to be its duty "to care for the welfare of all the Orthodox Churches which have been deprived of pastoral care,"[10] the Ecumenical Patriarch recognized the Churches of Finland (1923), Estonia

(1923), and Latvia (1936) as "autonomous" and the Church of Poland as "autocephalous" (1924).

The Russian Church considered all these acts as violations of its rights as a Mother Church, which, according to the views of the Moscow Patriarchate, alone could grant autonomous or autocephalous status to a Church separating from it. With the changed political situation later, the Patriarch of Moscow succeeded in depriving these acts of the Ecumenical Patriarch of their effectiveness. After the Second World War, the democratic republics of Estonia and Latvia became Union Republics of the USSR, and their Churches were reunited with the Russian Church as its dioceses and lost their autonomy.

The effectiveness of Constantinople's grant of autocephalous status to the Church of Poland was nullified in another way. The Polish democratic government, which favored autocephalous status for the Polish Church, was replaced (after the Second World War) by a government friendly to the Communist government of the USSR. The Moscow Patriarch thereupon proclaimed Metropolitan Dionysius, the acting head of the Polish autocephalous Church, suspended from his office and deprived of liturgical and canonical communion with the Russian Church to which he had formerly belonged. The administration of the Orthodox Church in Poland was assumed by a "Governing Board" of a few bishops. According to a petition of this Board, the Moscow Patriarch, in agreement with the Council of Russian Bishops, granted, "by the authority of the Mother Church," complete autocephalous status, instead of the "uncanonical and invalid autocephalous status" proclaimed by the Tomos of the Patriarch of Constantinople. Athenagoras, the Patriarch of Constantinople, sought to regard the grant of autocephalous status by the Moscow Patriarch as a recognition of the 1924 act of the Church of Constantinople, and therefore proposed to reestablish Metropolitan Dionysius in his rights. But the Patriarch of Moscow did not accept this proposal. Referring to the right of the Mother Church, the Patriarch of Moscow denied the authority of the Ecumenical Patriarch to grant autocephalous status to a Church which previously was not under the jurisdiction of the Church of Constantinople. The rejection went so far that the autocephalous status granted to the Polish Church "by a foreign Patriarch" was declared completely invalid.

Continuing to develop the same idea of the prerogatives of the Mother Church, the Moscow Patriarchate recognized the autocephalous status of the Church of Czechoslovakia in 1951. This status was proclaimed by the Moscow Patriarchate without any previous consultation with the Ecumenical Patriarch. Nevertheless, the Czechoslovakian Church was later recognized not only by the Churches behind the Iron Curtain, but also by the Patriarchal Sees of Alexandria and Antioch.

More serious disagreements arose between the Patriarchate of Constantinople and other autocephalous Churches about the reestablishment of the Bulgarian Patriarchate. In this case, many Local Churches opposed the will of the Patriarch of Constantinople. The Bulgarian Church, after having been granted autocephalous status by the Patriarch of Constantinople in 1945, decided to proclaim the restoration of the Patriarchate on its own initiative. To receive recognition of its new status by all the other Orthodox Local Churches, the Holy Synod of the Bulgarian Church invited their representatives to take part in the enthronement of the new Patriarch of the Bulgarian Church. The Ecumenical Patriarch received such an invitation as well. At the appointed time representatives of the Local Churches arrived in Sofia, but there was no representative from Constantinople. Soon a letter arrived from Athenagoras, the Ecumenical Patriarch, in which "the attributing to herself of patriarchal dignity and honor by the Bulgarian Church on her own accord" was considered "a deviation from the existing canonical and ecclesiastical order." According to this letter, the Bulgarian Church had to "seek her elevation to the Patriarchal dignity through us" (the Ecumenical Patriarchal See) from the body of the presiding Heads of the Holy Orthodox Churches. Besides, the letter made it clear that in passing on this application, the Ecumenical Patriarch would consider whether the Bulgarian Church had reached maturity and had manifested its constancy and loyalty to canonical principles.[11] In spite of the refusal at first of the Ecumenical Patriarch to recognize the Patriarchate of Bulgaria, it was recognized by the Patriarchs of the Churches of Alexandria, Antioch, and Jerusalem, as well as by the Churches of communist countries—Russia, Romania, Georgia, Poland, and Czechoslovakia—that is, by the majority of the existing Local Churches.[12] (In 1961, the Ecumenical Patriarch also did recognize the Bulgarian Patriarchate.)

The prerogatives of the Mother Church to grant autocephalous status did not receive unconditional universal recognition. The autocephalous status of the Polish and Czechoslovak Churches granted to them by their Russian Mother Church was not recognized by the Churches of Constantinople, Greece, or Cyprus.

Despite its insistence upon the prerogatives of the Mother Church, the Moscow Patriarchate itself sometimes acted against the interests of other Mother Churches and thereby weakened this principle. In 1937 the Albanian Church received autocephalous status from its Mother Church, Constantinople. However, the Moscow Patriarchate maintained relations not with the Holy Synod established according to the Statute of 1937, but with the bishops friendly to the communist government of Albania. Later, with the consent of the government, a new Synod, consisting of these bishops, replaced the Holy Synod which had originated on the basis of the Statute approved by the Church of Constantinople. The Moscow Patriarchate recognized the new Head of the Albanian Church, but the Patriarch of Constantinople refused to recognize him and did not enter into canonical communion with him. In addition, the interests of the Serbian Patriarchate were also impaired by the Moscow Patriarchate. Some of the parishes in Czechoslovakia which were under the jurisdiction of the Serbian Church fell under the authority of the Patriarch of Moscow in 1945. This gave rise to the displeasure of the Serbian Church. In 1951 these parishes were included in the new autocephalous Church of Czechoslovakia.

Although the collision of two systems of recognition weakened both of them, the growing number of Local Churches and the strengthening of their mutual relations stressed the specific need to have a "first" among members to whom others could apply for advice in their difficulties, and who could promote common action by all the Sister Churches. The appeals of the Churches of Finland, Estonia, Latvia, Poland, and of the Russian Metropolitan District of Western Europe, to the Ecumenical Patriarch after World War I indicate the high prestige of the Ecumenical Patriarch in the Orthodox Church. Regarding the Church of Finland, the Moscow Patriarchate, in 1958, could not but recognize its autonomy, granted by the Ecumenical Patriarch, although this was done in complete disagreement with the claims of the Moscow Patriarchate concerning the prerogatives of the Mother Church.

As practice has evolved, the recognition of a new Church and its introduction into the community of Orthodox Local Churches is now decided not by one Mother Church nor by the Ecumenical Patriarch in Constantinople alone, but by all the autocephalous Local Churches together. They reserve the right to accept or disapprove the decision of the Mother Church or the Ecumenical Patriarch. Autonomous or autocephalous status of a church, has been recognized by Local Churches without previous approval as well as the patriarchal dignity of an autocephalous church, of either the Ecumenical Patriarch (as in the cases of Bulgaria, Czechoslovakia, and Albania) or the Mother Church (as in Poland, Finland, Estonia, and Latvia). From the jurisdiction of a single Local Church this problem is coming to be decided by all the Local Churches, and thus the ancient principle of deciding this matter by the whole community of autocephalous Churches is being revived. The recognition by the Mother Church can, of course, facilitate the later recognition by other Local Churches, but, under present circumstances, the problem of which Church has the right to decide in the first instance loses its sharpness. Sometimes the Local Churches recognized a new Church after its Mother Church granted it autocephalous status, sometimes the Ecumenical Patriarch was the first to act. The Bulgarian Church was elevated to the Patriarchal dignity by many Churches without previous recognition by either the Ecumenical Patriarch or the Mother Church, both being represented by the same Church of Constantinople. The appeal of the Bulgarian Church was forwarded not to the Mother Church nor to the Ecumenical Patriarch but to all autocephalous Churches simultaneously. In this manner a new way of initiating a request for recognition was shown.

The system of recognition of new Churches by each particular Local Church is much slower than the system of recognition by an Ecumenical Council. Individual Local Churches may not be recognized for some time by all the autocephalous Churches. However, in time, the Orthodox Sister Churches may drop their objections, as was done in connection with the Church of Finland in 1958; and, when, in 1960, the Ecumenical Patriarch recognized the autocephalous Church of Poland and, in 1961, the Patriarchate of Bulgaria.

VII

THE PROCLAMATION OF ITS OWN
INDEPENDENCE BY A NEW CHURCH

Obstacles to the recognition of a new Church and unsuc-
cessful attempts to obtain recognition from the Mother
Church have usually resulted in a Church itself proclaiming
its own independence. If the proclamation is given practical
effect, that Church becomes, *de facto*, independent and
self-governing, enjoying the rights of an autocephalous
Church.

There are very few examples of a Mother Church granting autonomous or autocephalous status to a subsisting part
of itself in a comparatively short time. (This did occur,
though, when the Ecumenical Patriarch granted autonomy,
and later autocephaly, to the Serbian Church in 1832 and
1879 respectively.) In the past, the founding of a new
Church occurred mostly without the consent of the Mother
Church; canonical relations were usually broken off and
sometimes the new Church was even excommunicated.
Later, however, there was no alternative for the Mother
Church but to recognize the independence of the separated
Church. The Patriarch of Constantinople, for example, had
to recognize the self-proclaimed independence of the following Churches in the nineteenth and twentieth centuries:
the Church of Greece in 1850, 17 years after it had proclaimed itself autocephalous; the Romanian Church in
1885, 20 years after; the Albanian Church in 1937, 15 years

after; and the Bulgarian Church in 1945, 72 years after. In the fourteenth century the Serbian Church was recognized by the Patriarch of Constantinople 30 years after it had proclaimed itself independent (1346, 1375), and in the sixteenth century the Russian Church—140 years after (1448-1589). In the twentieth century the Patriarch of Moscow recognized the Finnish Church 35 years after it had been granted autonomy by the Ecumenical Patriarch (1923-1958).

The Mother Church usually regarded separation from itself as arbitrary and uncanonical. It must, nevertheless, be noted that even the largest Local Churches had to use the same arbitrary methods when separating from the Church of Constantinople. This historical fact deprives them, in turn, of any right to condemn similar "arbitrary" separations of their own parts. We might expect that these Churches later regretted their previous action and even condemned it now; but they did and do not. On the contrary, the declaration of its own independence by a new Church was recognized by the Conference of the Heads and Representatives of the Autocephalous Orthodox Churches in Moscow in 1948. This Conference was convened on the invitation of Alexis, the Patriarch of Moscow, "on the occasion of the celebration of the 500th anniversary of the autocephaly of the Russian Orthodox Church."

In 1448 the Council of Bishops of the Russian Church, which until that time had been one of the metropolitan districts of the Church of Constantinople, elected the Russian Bishop Jonah as the Metropolitan of Moscow, without seeking the approval of the Patriarch of Constantinople, and thereby laid the basis for the self-government and independence of the Russian Church. Although the Russian Church was canonically recognized by the Church of Constantinople only in 1589, Alexis, the Patriarch of Moscow, dates the beginning of the autocephaly not from the time of this canonical recognition, but from the year when the Russian Church proclaimed its own independence against the will of the Church of Constantinople.

It is also important to emphasize that Metropolitan Germanos, the Exarch of the Ecumenical Patriarch in Western Europe, stressed in his speech at the 1948 Conference that the Ecumenical Patriarch and his Holy Synod "received with utmost joy the decision of the great Russian Church to celebrate the 500th anniversary of its autocephaly." From the viewpoint of the representative of the Ecumenical Patriarch, the autocephaly of the Russian Church does date from the time (1448) it proclaimed itself independent. The Patriarchs of the Serbian and Romanian Churches and the Exarch of the Bulgarian Church participated in the celebration. They all congratulated the Russian Church on the 500th anniversary of its autocephaly and independence. Greetings were also conveyed from the Patriarch of Antioch, the Catholicos-Patriarch of the Church of Georgia, as well as from representatives of the Churches of Poland and Albania.[13] In this manner, a proclamation of its own canonical independence by a new Church, without the consent of its Mother Church, was accepted as lawful by the Russian Church as well as by representatives of the Ecumenical Patriarch and all the other autocephalous Churches attending the Moscow Conference of 1948. The real meaning of this acceptance can be properly understood if we remember the words of Patriarch Alexis during the general session of the Conference, where he declared that before the election of Metropolitan Jonah in 1448, the Russian Church "possessed all the canonical prerequisites... for autocephalous status." Therefore, the proclamation of independence may be made by a newly organized Church only if it meets all the usual requirements necessary for obtaining autocephalous status by other means.

The lack of formal recognition of a new Church did not prevent some Sister Churches from maintaining liturgical and canonical communion with it. After the Russian Church had proclaimed its independence from the Church of Constantinople, its relations with the Eastern Patriarchates were broken, but not for long. Soon they were reestablished. The connection of Moscow with Eastern Patriarchs was evidenced in its correspondence with them, in their letters and information about the personnel changes in the Patriarchates, in their repeated visits to Moscow, and in financial assistance by Moscow to the needy Churches of the East. The establishment of the Russian Patriarchate and the enthronement of the Russian Patriarch in 1589 took place during one such visit of the Eastern Patriarchs to Moscow. Although not recognized *de jure*, a new Church may enjoy *de facto* recognition by other autocephalous Local Churches.

VIII

THE AMERICAN DIOCESES OF THE ORTHODOX PATRIARCHATES IN EUROPE AND ASIA

After the First World War important changes occurred in the life of the Orthodox Church in America. Until that time the Russian Archdiocese of the Aleutian Islands and North America was the only branch of the Orthodox Church in America; some Greek, Serbian, Bulgarian, Romanian, and Syrian-Antiochian parishes were under its jurisdiction. In 1908 the Greek parishes were put under the control of the Church of Greece, but a Greek diocesan administration in America was not yet created. By the middle of the twentieth century there already were in the United States dioceses of five Patriarchates and, besides these, some purely national or local churches or ecclesiastical groups: Russian, Bulgarian, Romanian, Albanian, Ukranian, and Carpatho-Russian.

The five American dioceses of the Patriarchates located in Europe and Asia are the Greek Archdiocese of North and South America, the Syrian-Antiochian Orthodox Archdiocese of New York and all North America, the Patriarchal Exarchate of the Russian Orthodox Catholic Church in America, the Serbian Eastern Orthodox Diocese in America and the Romanian Orthodox Church in America. The Greek diocese was organized in 1918-1920, and in 1922 was placed under the jurisdiction of the Patriarch of Constantinople. Other dioceses were organized by their Mother

Churches, partly by uniting national parishes formerly included in the Russian Archdiocese. The Russian Archdiocese of the Aleutian Islands and North America became the independent Russian Orthodox Greek Catholic Church of America. The American Exarchate of the Moscow Patriarchate was later organized by Archbishop Benjamin, who was sent to New York in 1933 (Ukase of the Patriarchal Locum Tenens, Sergius, June 29, 1934, No. 1005).

Being American dependencies of Patriarchates whose headquarters lay outside America, the policies of all these dioceses have been subordinated to the direction of central bodies in Europe and Asia.

Difficult political conditions, especially Communist pressure through the central bodies of the Churches behind the Iron Curtain on their dioceses in the Western Hemisphere, have forced the latter to separate from their Mother Churches for the purpose of saving their religious freedom. Their purpose is sacred before God, but they should comply with canons and Church practice. The details of the canonical organization of these American parts of the Orthodox Local Churches abroad cannot be uniform for all of them. Their canonical status is to be established in conformity with their origin and their present state.

One of the most important problems of these ecclesiastical groups has been to secure a supply of duly appointed and consecrated bishops. Some of these groups in America were made up of only a few parishes, without a bishop, but desiring to establish a diocesan administration in the form of a national diocese or episcopate. After selecting a suitable candidate, they were obliged to ascertain whether, for the organization of a national diocese, it was canonically possible that their candidate be consecrated by canonical bishops of another Orthodox Church, and, if so, whether such a national ecclesiastical group could legitimately exist as an independent episcopate or diocese.

An Orthodox diocese exists only as a part of a Local Church which alone has the authority to consecrate new bishops for it. Only a candidate who has been duly appointed to the bishop's post may lawfully be consecrated. Canonical appointment means not only election by the people but also approbation by ruling bishops of the Orthodox Local Church. Since bishops may only appoint a new ruling bishop for a vacant diocesan seat of their own Church, and not of any other Local Church, appointment and consecration of a bishop for a petitioning group of parishes canonically may take place only after those parishes have joined some Local Church and been integrated into this Church as one of its dioceses. Hence, these Orthodox ecclesiastical groups can receive their own bishops lawfully only after they have submitted to and become incorporated into an existing Local Church. The Orthodox Canon Law does not recognize "independent dioceses."

The bishops of an Orthodox Local Church may consecrate a duly appointed candidate for bishop of another Orthodox Church only when they are requested to do so by the head of the other Orthodox Church. The newly consecrated bishop would then occupy one of the dioceses of the requesting Church. That occurs mostly when the Church does not have a sufficient number of bishops in the region where the consecration is to be performed. When they consecrate bishops for another Church, bishops of a Local Church act not on their own authority but on the invitation of the highest authorities of the other Church (Apostolic Canon 35; Antioch Canons 13, 22) and on behalf of this other Church.

Such an ecclesiastical group is the American Carpatho-Russian Orthodox Greek Catholic Church, which was largely organized from former Uniate groups. The Bishop of the Church—Orestes P. Chornok—was elected by a congress of the clergy and laity in 1937. Upon a special request, the Carpatho-Russian Church was later received under the jurisdiction of the Ecumenical Patriarch as the Carpatho-Russian Diocese in America. The election of Fr. Cbornok, therefore, legally constituted a recommendation only, which later was approved by the Ecumenical Patriarch and his Synod. Only then, after being canonically appointed by the authorities of the Church of Constantinople, could Fr. Chomok be consecrated as a bishop in Constantinople. Consequently, the American Carpatho-Russian Greek Catholic Church is not an independent Church, but only one of the dioceses of the Patriarchate of Constantinople, preserving certain historical and national features of this group.

In the same way, the Ukrainian ecclesiastical group headed by Bishop-elect Bohdan Shpilka was received in 1937 as an American diocese under the jurisdiction of the Patriarch of Constantinople, and then, by order of the Patriarch, Fr. Shpilka was consecrated bishop in New York by Archbishop Athenagoras of the Greek Archdiocese of North and South America. This group is now the Ukranian Orthodox Church of America.

In this connection, the large group of members of the Romanian Church must also be mentioned. The Romanian Episcopate in America was established by the Romanian Orthodox Patriarchate as early as 1930. From 1935 to 1939 the See was occupied by Bishop Policarp, who was approved by the Holy Synod of the Patriarchate of Romania. In 1939 Bishop Policarp went to Romania and was not able to return to America. Due to military and political circumstances, the Romanian Episcopate remained for many years without proper canonical ties with its Mother Church and was administered by local bodies. After the Communists seized power in Romania, a new bishop for America was appointed by the Patriarch of Romania, but the Congress of clergy and laity in America did not accept him. They severed all relationship with the Patriarch of Romania, and elected a new bishop, Valerian Trifa, L.Th. His consecration met with great difficulties. Finally he was consecrated by bishops of the Ukranian Orthodox Church of the United States of America. (This is not to be confused with the Ukranian Orthodox Church of America, mentioned above. The Ukranian Orthodox Church of the USA is the largest Ukranian ecclesiastical group in America. It is, however, in conflict with some recognized teachings of the Orthodox Church, especially that of the consecration to Holy Orders, and does not enjoy communion with other Orthodox Churches in America.) Besides the problem of the canonicity of these Ukranian bishops, it must also be taken into consideration that the Ukranian bishops had no right to consecrate a man to a diocese outside their own jurisdiction when he had not been duly appointed as a bishop by the bishops of the candidate's own Church. This uncanonical condition lasted until 1960 when, according to its own request, the Romanian Orthodox Episcopate was incorporated into the Russian Orthodox Greek Catholic Church of America by the decision of the latter's Bishops' Sobor as a Romanian Diocese with the preservation of the features of its self-government. Valerian Trifa, as the candidate for the diocesan See, nominated by the clergy and laity of the Romanian diocese, was approved by the Bishops' Sobor of the Russian Church of America and re-consecrated by the Metropolitan and Bishops of the Metropolitanate. First he had to pronounce the monastic vows and was made a monk; then he was ordained a deacon, subsequently a priest, and finally he was consecrated a bishop. Being canonically appointed and consecrated, Bishop Valerian became the canonical Head of the Romanian Diocese of the Russian Orthodox Church of America.

IX

THE RUSSIAN ORTHODOX CHURCH ABROAD

Among the new self-governing Orthodox Churches in America there are two which are of special importance: the Russian Orthodox Greek Catholic Church Abroad and the Russian Orthodox Greek Catholic Church of America (the American Metropolitanate).

1

Organized by refugee Russian bishops, the Russian Orthodox Church Abroad seeks to unite under its jurisdiction all Russian dioceses, ecclesiastical missions, and parishes located outside of Russia. It broke off relations with the present Moscow Patriarchate, considering it to be a Church deprived of freedom to express its own will or to exercise its canonical rights under the yoke of the godless Soviet Government. Essentially, the "Church of the Emigrés" is a temporary body, designed to last "until the restoration of normal conditions of social and ecclesiastical life in Russia."[14]

The Russian Orthodox Church Abroad recognizes no territorial limitations of its jurisdiction. In 1927, Metropolitan Anthony, Chairman of the Bishops' Synod in Karlovtsi, stated: "Neither the Sobor nor the Synod of Bishops is bound by any territory; if it becomes impossible to function in Serbia, they could continue their work in France, Germany, England, China, or any other state."[15] In fact, that is what happened. After becoming organized outside of Russia, the first seat of the Church Abroad was in Constantinople, subsequently transferred to Sremski Karlovtsi (Yugoslavia), Munich (Germany) and, finally, New York.

The Church Abroad was characterized not only by a refusal to recognize the Moscow Patriarchate, but also by profound canonical differences with the larger Russian ecclesiastical districts abroad, such as the West European and the American. Both these foreign parts of the Russian Church zealously adhered to the resolutions of the last Sacred Sobor of the Russian Church during 1917-18 in Moscow and worked to put them into practice, adjusting them to local conditions. The Moscow Sobor of 1917 restored the Patriarchate and reorganized the Russian Church on the ancient principles of conciliarity (*sobornost*) and self-government. At the same time it united bishops, clergymen, and parishioners at both central and local levels into one ecclesiastical body, preserving, however, the supremacy of the episcopate and the leadership of the clergy.

The hierarchy of the Church Abroad, on the other hand, found it impossible to reconcile itself with such clerical and lay activity in the central and local organs of Church administration. They repudiated these resolutions of the Sobor and reverted to the Russian Church system that prevailed before 1917. The Synod of Bishops, a small committee, was restored as the basic administrative organ, but, of course, without an "Ober-Procuror" appointed by the government. The Sobor, made up of all the Bishops, is regarded as the supreme ecclesiastical body. The Chairman of the Sobor of

Bishops is also the Chairman of the Synod of Bishops. Being a permanent institution, the Synod of Bishops is, in fact, the chief ruling body; therefore the Russian Orthodox Church Abroad is also known as the Synodal Church.

2

Attempts are naturally being made to justify canonically the existence of such an extraordinary ecclesiastical organization as the Russian Orthodox Church Abroad, which claims jurisdiction over all Russian Orthodox dioceses and parishes throughout the world outside of the Soviet Union.

First of all, the adherents of the Church Abroad pointed out that it had been recognized by the Ecumenical Patriarch and then by the Serbian Patriarch since its inception. However, the Ecumenical Patriarch allowed Russian emigre bishops to found only a temporary Church Committee in 1920 designed for the pastoral care of Russian refugees within the boundaries of the Church of Constantinople. The Committee enjoyed only limited powers. All attempts on the part of Russian bishops to expand their field of activity encountered resolute resistance by the patriarch. The Supreme Russian Church Administration Abroad founded by these Russian bishops was compelled to move to Sremski Karlovtsi (Yugoslavia) in 1921. Despite the extreme benevolence of the Serbian Patriarch toward them, the Council of Bishops of the Serbian Church resolved on August 18-31, 1921 to permit "independent organization and self-government" only "on the territory of the Serbian Church" and, at that, "under the protection and supervision of the Serbian Church."[16] Neither the Patriarch of Constantinople nor the Patriarch of Serbia could allow these Russian emigre bishops any

broader power than to administer Russian parishes within
their own territories. There is no reason to assume that the
claims of the bishops of Sremski Karlovtsi to authority over
the entire Russian Diaspora are based on the authority
granted to them by the Patriarch of Constantinople and of
Serbia. No Patriarch can grant any rights to bishops beyond
the jurisdiction of his own Church.

3

In view of the obvious inadequacy of the basis suppos-
edly furnished by the Ecumenical and the Serbian Patriarchs, the authority of the Bishops' Sobor and the Synod
was subsequently substantiated by the Ukase (No. 362) of
Patriarch Tikhon on November 20, 1920, which was declared the "basic law of the Church Abroad." This Ukase
granted authority to "diocesan bishops" to organize a
church administration whenever a diocese "would find
itself cut off from all communication with the Highest
Church Administration" or "when the Highest Church Administration, headed by the Holy Patriarch, would cease to
function." All measures which were taken pursuant to these
instructions were to be submitted to the Central Church Authority for confirmation after the reestablishment of the
latter. According to Article 2 of the Ukase, "...the diocesan
bishop shall forthwith communicate with the bishops of
neighboring dioceses for the purpose of organizing a supreme organ of Church authority for several dioceses in
which the same conditions prevail." The senior bishop in
that group was to take care of the organization of the administration for several dioceses (Article 3). The adherents of
the Church Abroad interpret these passages as an authority

given to the senior bishop outside Russia to organize a common administration for all Russian dioceses and parishes abroad in collaboration with other bishops.[17]

This viewpoint was subsequently adopted by the California Superior Court in Los Angeles in the case of *Russian Orthodox Church of the Transfiguration et al. vs. Rev. A. Lisin et al.* (decided November 29, 1948).[18] The Court said: "A fair reading of the Ukase in the light of the canons, the necessity that there be but one church with one head and the emergency which existed has caused the court to conclude that the Ukase was designed for the purpose of creating a supreme church administration for the whole Church throughout the world outside of the boundaries controlled by the Bolsheviks" (Memorandum of Opinion, p. 15).

Despite the California Court's assurances, a close study fails to reveal any adequate foundation for the claim that the Ukase sanctioned the creation of a Supreme Church Administration for all Russian dioceses and parishes outside the Soviet Union. The Ukase was promulgated as a result of the inevitable isolation of parts of the Church brought about by the shifting of the battlefront during the Civil War in Russia. The Ukase does, indeed, refer to the organization of a Church administration "in the form of a provisional Supreme Church Government," as a "metropolitan district" or "otherwise" (Article 2). It mentions the organization of an ecclesiastical government not only for "some neighboring dioceses" (Article 2) but even for one diocese (Article 4). The division of one diocese into several parts under the administration of vicar bishops is also anticipated (Article 5). Furthermore, several forms of ecclesiastical organization are indicated without, however, specifying a definite form or, in particular, the creation of one Church with one Head in the spirit of Roman Catholic Canon Law.

It is obvious that the Ukase of Patriarch Tikhon promulgated in 1920 in no way represented an authorization for the Russian emigre bishops in Karlovtsi to create an ecclesiastical administration abroad, inasmuch as it did not even apply to them. It was addressed to "diocesan bishops," i.e. the bishops in charge of a particular diocese. It was concerned primarily with the dioceses of the Russian Church in Russia and the dioceses outside it—if they had been founded by the authority of the Russian Church. However, the emigre bishops who had fled their dioceses in Russia were no longer heads of these dioceses. There was no "diocese" in either Serbia or Bulgaria created before the Revolution by the Church Authority in Russia. None of the bishops was appointed by such Authority in Russia to Sremski Karlovtsi or Sofia. The Russian bishops and their parishes within the jurisdiction of the Serbian Patriarchate were merely a self-governing ecclesiastical group under the protection and supervision of the Patriarch of the Serbian Church and, thus, an integral part of the Serbian Patriarchate. Being under the jurisdiction of the Serbian Patriarchate and retaining self-government, this national group did not form a territorial diocese of the Serbian Church, neither was it a diocese of the Russian Church.

In view of the complications which arise in the application of the 1920 Ukase to the group of bishops in Karlovtsi and their parishes, which from a canonical standpoint were not a diocese of the Russian Church, the advocates of the

Church Abroad insist that that group "has to be considered a 'diocese'." Fr. Polsky wonders why the newly formed "emigre diocese" in the Balkans should not be called a diocese: "How then could dioceses be founded abroad in the past, and if so, why may they not be founded now?"[19] The answer is obvious: because a diocese as an administrative division of a Church can be organized only by the central authorities of the same Church and the bishops of this diocese are to be appointed by the authorities of the same Church. In a new country, emigre bishops are not empowered to organize a diocese of the Church from which they had withdrawn. From a canonical viewpoint they were under the jurisdiction of the Patriarch of another Church who did not have the power to create a new administrative division of the Russian Church outside its boundaries, any more than they themselves could have done it.

The applicability of the 1920 Ukase to the Karlovtsi group of bishops has become even more questionable in the course of further developments: the dismissal of the Highest Church Administration Abroad by the Ukase of Patriarch Tikhon, dated May 5, 1922; the transfer by the same Patriarch of the administration of Russian parishes abroad to Metropolitan Eulogius; the new abolition of the Highest Church Administration in Karlovtsi by order of Metropolitan Sergius, dated May 9, 1928; and the discontinuation of all administrative relations with Moscow. The Los Angeles case of the Transfiguration Church (referred to above) reveals also that the Superior Court of the State of California did not attach any decisive importance to the 1920 Ukase. It was merely considered by the Court as an "additional basis for the creation and existence of the Supreme Church Administration of the Church Abroad" (Memorandum of opinion, p. 15). It is evident that the Patriarchal Ukase of 1920 cannot be the basic law of the Church Abroad in any event.

4

The significance of the Ukase of 1920 has been overshadowed by another idea of the adherents of the Church Abroad; according to this idea, the Orthodox bishops, as such, having been forced to leave Russia, are empowered to govern all dioceses and parishes of the Russian Church located outside of Russia and have the right to organize a Supreme Church Administration.[20] This idea received a great deal of emphasis in subsequent defenses of the canonical status of the Church Abroad.

The apologists of the Church Abroad take particular pleasure in emphasizing that the Superior Court of the State of California has fully recognized this authority of the Sobor and Synod of Bishops in Karlovtsi. In fact, the above-discussed decision of the Los Angeles Court is based on the principle that, according to canons, "...the ultimate power and duty to rule the Church has been placed in the hands of bishops (for instance, Apostolic Canon 34 and Antioch 9)." From this proposition the following conclusion was made in accordance with the views of the Church Abroad: "When the Church in Russia was completely disorganized and the supreme administration was destroyed, under the canons it became the duty of the surviving bishops who were not imprisoned to gather together and create a supreme Church administration. This was an absolute necessity if order was to prevail. This is what the bishops who gathered together at Karlovtsi in the year 1921 did" (Memorandum of Opinion, pp. 12, 13).

However, the canons specify that the authority to rule the Church is not granted to persons in the rank of bishop but to those of them only who are appointed by the Supreme Church Authority to the see of a definite diocese. A clear-cut distinction is made in the canons between bishops who rule dioceses and those who do not.

According to Canons 4 and 5 of the First Ecumenical Council and the above-mentioned Canon 9 of the Council of Antioch, a bishop could be a member of the Provincial Council of Bishops only if he ruled one of the dioceses of the Province. The ruling bishops alone took part in the administration of the Church because the so-called absolute ordinations, that is, without appointment to a Church, were declared invalid (Canon 6, Fourth Ecumenical Council). A bishop could be ordained after he was designated to a bishopric (Canon 4, First Ecumenical Council). A retired bishop had the right to retain his rank and dignity but no longer enjoyed any of the rights of administration and was allowed to act only by permission of the ruling bishop of the diocese to which he belonged (Letter of the Holy Council of Ephesus to the Sacred Council in Pamphilia). The canons recognize the right to administer and participate in the Council of Bishops exclusively for ruling bishops. These regulations were subsequently adopted by the Russian Church.

Among the fifteen bishops who participated in the 1921 Council at Karlovtsi,[21] only one was a ruling bishop of a diocese founded by the Russian Church, namely Bishop Eulogius, whose jurisdiction comprised the West European district of the Russian Church. The bishops who attended the Council in Karlovtsi used the names of their former dioceses, *e.g.*, Bishop of Kieve, Poltava, Kursk, Kherson, Kishinev, Cheliabinsk, etc. The use of these titles, which were no longer in force, only served to emphasize that their bearers had no dioceses under their Jurisdiction. Being nonruling bishops, they had no right to participate in a Council of Bishops which could adopt resolutions affecting Church administration. Therefore, because of its composition, the Karlovtsi Sobor of 1921 was not canonically able to make decisions concerning the organization and administration of the Church; furthermore, the bishops who attended the Sobor were not empowered to established a new Church.

While emphasizing the bishops' right to organize the Supreme Church Administration, the adherents of the Synodal Church, in reality, proclaim the power of bishops to establish a self-governing church. Their point of view has also been adopted by the Superior Court of the State of California in Los Angeles. The Court regarded the Bishops' Sobor and Bishops' Synod as "the supreme legislative, judicial and administrative authority over the Church Abroad and over all members of the Church outside of Russia and all its dioceses and all its parishes, with full power and jurisdiction over all questions of a general ecclesiastical nature" (Findings of fact and conclusions of law, XIV, p. 42). The creation of such ecclesiastical bodies by the Karlovtsi Sobor in 1921 could not be other than an attempt to establish a new Orthodox Church.

According to the canonical principles and the practice of the Orthodox Church, a new self-governing Church cannot be founded by a simple mutual consent of individual bishops. It can only be formed from a foreign part of an Autocephalous Church with at least three duly appointed *ruling* bishops. Although the number of bishops who attended the Sobor in Karlovtsi exceeded three by far, none of them (with the exception of Archbishop Eulogius) had been appointed by the Supreme Authority of the Russian Church in Moscow to rule a foreign diocese which belonged to the Russian Church. The basic part of the Church Abroad—the parishes in Serbia and Bulgaria ruled by Russian emigre bishops—was not a diocese previously instituted by the Russian Church. At the time, neither the West European nor the North American Districts intended to separate themselves from the Russian Church. The "new Church" formed by the bishops residing at Karlovtsi did not represent a branch that sprang from the tree of the Orthodox Church, but was a newly-planted tree. Only by ignoring the concept of the Orthodox Church as one tree with branches could the Church Abroad have been founded by the group of Karlovtsi bishops without dioceses. Consequently, neither the Bishops' Sobor nor the Bishops' Synod created in 1921 was canonically authorized to found and rule over a new Orthodox Church.

It also turned out that the claim of the Bishops' Synod in Karlovtsi to the rule over all Russian dioceses and parishes outside the Soviet Union was an intrusion into the jurisdiction of the Russian Orthodox Church itself.[22] The Bishops' Synod in Karlovtsi not only claimed jurisdiction over the parishes in Serbia and Bulgaria but also over the West European district and the North American diocese of the Russian Church. The West European district was originally under the jurisdiction of the vicar bishop of the Metropolitan of St Petersburg. The North American diocese had belonged to the Russian Church for over a hundred years. Despite his very delicate situation, Patriarch Tikhon, with the Holy Synod in Moscow, continued to appoint ruling bishops to these dioceses. On April 8, 1921, Archbishop Eulogius was appointed to rule over all Churches in Western Europe and in 1922 received the rank of Metropolitan from Patriarch Tikhon, with the authority to rule over all Russian parishes throughout Europe. At the same time, Platon, former Metropolitan of Kherson and Odessa, was appointed head of the North American Diocese, also by Patriarch Tikhon, on April 27, 1922.[23] Although the Russian Metropolitan Districts in Western Europe and America enjoyed a large degree of self-government by virtue of the Patriarchal Ukase of 1920, they remained parts of the Russian Church at the time of the Karlovtsi Sobor and for some time thereafter.

Inasmuch as the resolutions of the Karlovtsi Sobor of 1921 and of the Synod, accepted by the majority vote of the emigre bishops, concerned the subjugation of dioceses which canonically were still part of the Russian Church, they could not have had any canonical validity. Interference with the life of another Church is strictly forbidden (Apostolic Canons 34, 35; Second Ecumenical Council, Canon 2; Antioch Council, Canons 9, 13). The Bishops' Sobor and Synod in Karlovtsi were not authorized canonically to extend their power to cover the foreign dioceses of the Russian Church; they could not dismiss bishops legally appointed by the Supreme Authorities of the Russian Church; neither were they authorized to appoint new bishops or priests for these dioceses, establish new parishes, or summon the clergymen of these dioceses before the ecclesiastical courts and impose ecclesiastical punishments.

According to the Orthodox viewpoint, bishops are created by the Church, appointed and consecrated, and they cannot organize a new Church on their own motion, especially in another country outside the boundaries of the Church from which they had fled, thereby losing their dioceses. A new Orthodox Church cannot be organized as a human society. It can only be an offspring of the majestic tree of the whole Church, which had been founded by Christ and His Apostles many hundred years ago.

The Superior Court of the State of California, in the suit about the Church of the Transfiguration, acted under the assumption that the foundation of the Church Abroad was the duty of the bishops abroad and absolutely necessary for the preservation of order under conditions that prevailed at the time. However, nobody can be obliged to do what he has no right to do. The former ruling bishops who gathered in Karlovtsi had no canonical right to establish a new Church. Any measure that seems to be necessary in practice may be given legal approval only if it is permissible under the law.

Inasmuch as the jurisdiction of the Local Orthodox Churches is territorially delimited,[24] a group of Orthodox Christians who come to another Local Church to live within its territory has to submit to the authorities of this Church. A self-governing organization may be formed only in countries where there is no Local Orthodox Church. Metropolitan Sergius indicated such a possible solution of the problem "on the basis of canon law" in a letter dated September 12, 1926, to the bishops of the Church Abroad. At that time, there was no canonical need for the establishment of a new superterritorial Church Abroad. The Russian dioceses in Western Europe, the Far East, and America had a duly appointed hierarchy authorized to continue the administration of their dioceses independently, particularly by virtue of the Ukase of Patriarch Tikhon of November 20, 1920. Problems might have arisen only as to the coordination of their activities. The bishops in Karlovtsi were acting canonically only when they sought to organize an "emigre diocese" with the permission of the Serbian Church, within its boundaries only. But the foundation of a self-governing Russian Church Abroad and the claim to have all Russian dioceses, missions, and parishes outside the Soviet Union under its jurisdiction cannot be justified either by the canons or the practices of the Orthodox Church.

5

In order to substantiate the claims of the Bishops' Sobor and Synod to the jurisdiction over the American Metropolitanate, the adherents of the Church Abroad refer to the "participation in one way or another" of the American Metropolitanate in "nearly all actions"[25] relevant to the establishment of the Church Abroad. It seems necessary to provide a clearer definition for such ambiguous words as "nearly" or "in one way or another" so as to determine the purpose for and the conditions under which the representatives of the American Metropolitanate participated in the organs of the Church Abroad.

The 1921 Sobor in Karlovtsi, at which the Supreme Church Administration of the Church Abroad was established, was not attended by any representative of the North

American Metropolitanate; the latter joined the organization later on through correspondence. Metropolitan Platon did attend the Sobor as former ruling bishop of Kherson and Odessa, but he was not appointed to the North American Diocese by Patriarch Tikhon until 1922. As the head of this diocese Metropolitan Platon took part in the affairs of the Church Abroad during the later period from 1922 to 1926. The fact that he attended the sessions of the Bishops' Sobor and Synod certainly did not mean that he considered himself subordinate to these bodies in the administration of his own district.

As an appointee of the central authority of the Russian Church to one of its dioceses, there was no reason for Metropolitan Platon to consider himself subordinate to the Bishops' Synod Abroad. His only reason for participating in the sessions was to coordinate the activity of the American Metropolitan District with that of other districts of the Russian Church which were not subordinate one to another, such as the West European District, the "emigre diocese" in the Near East and the Far Eastern District. Both Metropolitan Platon and Metropolitan Eulogius were fully entitled to withdraw from the Bishops' Synod in their capacity as heads of dioceses independent from the Synod and did so in 1926 as soon as the Karlovtsi group of bishops began to subjugate other districts, instead of keeping within its coordinating function. The Bishops' Synod, being displeased with the measures taken by Metropolitan Platon in the administration of the American Metropolitanate, suspended him from his office and even barred him from performing Divine Services. These measures were just as ineffective as if a retired bishop had tried to appoint or depose clergymen in a neighboring diocese.

6

By way of argument in favor of the Church Abroad, it is pointed out that the American Metropolitanate recognized the highest authorities of the Church Abroad and fully subordinated itself to the Provisional Statute on the Russian Orthodox Church Abroad adopted "by all bishops and parts of the Church Abroad, by Metropolitan Theophilus as Head" of the American Metropolitan District, and by this "organization itself and its representatives." Pursuant to this Provisional Statute, the American Metropolitanate is to be considered—according to the decision of December 31, 1948, of the California Superior Court—"reunited and merged" with the Church Abroad, as "an integral part of the Church Abroad, subject to its jurisdiction, government, and laws...on the same basis as other dioceses of the Church Abroad," so that secession from the Church Abroad could only have been "effected with express approval of the governing organ of the Church Abroad," that is, of the Bishops' Sobor (Findings of fact and conclusions of law XIX, XX, pp. 45-47, 54-55).

The above statements with regard to the legal position of the American Metropolitanate were based on the assumption that the Provisional Statute became binding for the American Metropolitanate in the wording accepted by the Bishops' Sobor at Karlovtsi in 1935.[26] But this Statute could come into effect only after its approval by the supreme bodies of both parties. The approval of the text of the Provisional Statute by the Bishops' Sobor of the Synodal Church at Karlovtsi could not make the Statute binding for the American Metropolitanate. The American Metropolitan who attended the Sobor sessions could not by himself impose his agreement with the Karlovtsi bishops upon the whole American Metropolitanate. Since the Detroit Sobor of 1924, the American Metropolitanate was ruled by the Metropolitan jointly with the Bishops' Sobor, the Metropolitan Council, and the periodically convened Sobor of the whole American Church. The task of the All American Sobor, consisting of bishops, clergymen and laymen, was to elect the Metropolitan and to settle basic organizational problems of the Church. The American Metropolitanate could not be united with the Russian dioceses abroad without the approval of the Statute by the All American Sobor. The Sixth All American Sobor of 1937 in New York adopted the 1935 Provisional Statute subject to certain "adjustments to local conditions of the [American Metropolitan] District." Some important amendments were introduced so that some sections of the Provisional Statute of 1935 could not come into effect in their original form. Therefore, the real nature of agreement between the American Metropolitanate and the Church Abroad can properly be evaluated in the light of the resolutions adopted by the Sixth All American Sobor in 1937 and not only on the basis of the original text of the Provisional Statute of 1935.[27]

First of all, the change of Section IX, 1, of the Provisional Statute is to be mentioned. According to this section the diocesan bishops had the right to appoint and transfer the parish priests by their own authority. But the Statute of the North American Metropolitan District, accepted by the All American Sobor at the same time as the Provisional Statute, established on the contrary that the appointment and transfer of the parish priests were to be made by the

metropolitan of the American District, in concurrence with
the diocesan bishop. Later on this regulation was amended
by the District Sobor of Bishops, against the will of the
American Metropolitan Theophilus. The Metropolitan's
right to transfer clergymen from one diocese to another was
preserved, but the diocesan bishops were authorized to appoint and transfer clergymen within the boundaries of their
dioceses with subsequent information of the Metropolitan.
Practically, the appointment and transfer of priests were
made, with only some exceptions, by Metropolitan
Theophilus himself, who was supported in this respect for
the most part by the clergymen of the Metropolitanate.

Furthermore, by the same Statute of the North American
Metropolitan District, the Metropolitan Council of clergymen and laymen was reestablished. This Council had functioned since 1924, but was totally omitted from the
Provisional Statute. The Sixth All American Sobor made an
addition to Sections VI, VII, and VIII of the Provisional
Statute by including the Metropolitan Council in the
number of administrative bodies of the American Metropolitan District. After 1937, the Metropolitan Council continued to function on the basis of the resolutions of the All
American Sobor alone.

The most important change of the Provisional Statute
was the preservation of the All American Sobor, vested with
the power to resolve the problems of Church organization by
virtue of its own authority. Being one of the higher organs of
Church administration and comprising bishops, clergymen
and laymen as its members, the All American Sobor was not
acceptable to the bishops of the Synodal Church. As early as

1926, the Bishops' Synod insisted that Metropolitan Platon disapprove the resolutions of the Detroit Sobor on the order of administration of the Church in America. However, the Metropolitan refused to do so. The Provisional Statute of 1935 was directed mainly against the very existence of an All American Sobor which included clergymen and laymen. Like the Metropolitan Council, such a Sobor was not even mentioned in the Provisional Statute. According to this Statute, all problems concerning amendments or additions to the Statute were to be settled only by the Bishops' Sobor of the Church Abroad (Section III, 9), and the Provisional Statute itself was in no case to be submitted for consideration or approval to the All American Sobor. However, the bishops of the American Metropolitanate insisted at the Bishops' Conference in May 1936, that the regular American Sobor be convoked and that "...upon approval by this Sobor and in collaboration and contact with it...certain amendments and additions be introduced to the Provisional Statute" according to the local conditions of the North American district. The bishops appointed by the Karlovtsi Synod also attended that Conference and advocated the convocation of an American Sobor, considering it a "general Diocesan Convention,"[28] although the latter was also not anticipated by the Provisional Statute. The convocation of that Sobor was in reality a violation of the Provisional Statute of 1935, which specified that any changes or amendments could only be introduced by the Bishops' Sobor of the Church Abroad.

During the sessions of the All American Sobor of 1937, the bishops appointed by the Bishops' Synod Abroad requested that the amendments adopted by the Sobor be sub-

mitted to the Bishops' Sobor Abroad for approval, but the
All American Sobor rejected this suggestion. At the end of
its sessions, when the proposal was raised to submit the resolutions to the Bishops' Sobor Abroad for approval, the
Sobor resolved to submit all its resolutions to the Bishops'
Sobor of the Church Abroad for its "information" only and
not for "approval."[29] Accordingly the resolutions were sent
by Metropolitan Theophilus to the President of the
Bishops' Sobor and Synod "for information" only. Thus the
decision of the All American Sobor of 1937 means that,
contrary to the Provisional Statute of 1935, the All American Sobor retained the right to continue making decisions
on the organization of the American Metropolitanate by its
own authority, and without submitting these resolutions to
the Bishops' Sobor of the Church Abroad for approval. By
this action the All American Sobor showed that it refused to
accept Section III, 9, of the Provisional Statute, by which
the exclusive right to make amendments and additions to
the Provisional Statute rested with the Bishops' Sobor of
the Church Abroad. A mutual agreement was not reached
on this subject, and, thus, the Section III, 9, cannot be considered binding.

In its decision of January 3, 1938, regarding the resolutions of the Sixth All American Sobor, the Bishops' Sobor
of the Church Abroad[30] did not abrogate and did not declare
ineffective the inclusion of the All American Sobor in the
scheme of the higher bodies of the American Metropolitan
District. It insisted only that, according to Section III, 9, of
the Provisional Statute, the resolutions of the All American
Sobor could be valid only after their approval by the
Bishops' Sobor of the Church Abroad. But this claim could

not be based on Section III, 9, because this section itself could not be considered effective.

In his letter of November 16, 1937, to the President of the Bishops' Sobor, Metropolitan Anastasius, Metropolitan Theophilus asserted that the All American Sobor had not been under obligation to send its resolutions to the Bishops' Sobor for approval, because the Statute mentioned the approval of resolutions of the District Sobors of the diocesan bishops only, but not those of the All American Sobor (Section VIII, 2). Metropolitan Theophilus was right insofar as the All American Sobor was not even mentioned in the Provisional Statute and continued to exist outside the resolutions of this Provisional Statute, preserving its right to resolve administrative problems independently of the supreme bodies of the Church Abroad.

Using this right, the Seventh All American Sobor in Cleveland (1946) dissolved the union with the Church Abroad. In order to reinforce the self-government of the American Metropolitanate, it revoked any subordination to the Synod Abroad and appealed to the Moscow Patriarch for recognition of the "full autonomy" of the Church in America. This decision is considered ineffective by the California Superior Court because it was not submitted for approval to, and was not approved by, the higher organs of the Church Abroad, that is, the Bishops' Sobor or Synod, in accordance with the Provisional Statute. However, the opinion of the Court that the resolutions of the All American Sobor should be approved by the Bishops' Sobor of the Church Abroad cannot be based on the Provisional Statute amended by the Sixth All American Sobor, for the reasons given above.

The question arises, however, as to why the decision of the Seventh All American Sobor to end its relationship with the Church Abroad was not submitted for approval to the bishops who attended the Sobor, although a rule to that effect was promulgated by Metropolitan Theophilus in his "Instruction" prior to the holding of the Sobor. During the course of the sessions this provision was changed by the Sobor, which resolved that its decisions not be submitted for the approval of the Bishops' Conference. According to the Los Angeles Superior Court in December 1948, this was a violation of the right of the Bishops' Conference and, along with a failure to submit the resolutions to the Bishops' Sobor of the Church Abroad for approval, made these resolutions wholly invalid (Findings of fact and conclusions of law XXVII, pp. 51, 52).

But a violation of the rules of procedure may invalidate a resolution only if such violation substantially leads to the adoption of the resolution. In this case, however, the resolution of the Sobor—accepted without submitting it to the Bishops' Conference for approval—would have been approved unchanged if it had been submitted to that Conference. The All American Sobor of 1946 was attended by nine bishops only. One of them, Bishop Seraphim, was there only as a guest and had no right to vote. Four bishops belonged to the Karlovtsi group and were against the resolution of the Sobor, while the other four, headed by Metropolitan Theophilus, supported it. In the case of a tie the deciding vote is usually cast by the president. Metropolitan Theophilus was the president of both the Sobor and the Conference of Bishops. Therefore, the decisive vote would have been that of the group of supporters of the resolution to which the Metropolitan belonged.[31] From the very beginning of the sessions two irreconcilable groups of bishops emerged at the Sobor. Whether the resolutions of the Sobor were discussed or not by the Bishops' Conference, the Karlovtsi Bishops would not have been able to vote down the resolution to end the relationship between the American Metropolitanate and the Church Abroad. Such discussion would not have had an issue favorable to them in any event. Were it to have taken place, the resolution of the Sobor would have been approved by the votes of the four bishops of the American Metropolitanate headed by Metropolitan Theophilus with whose consent it was put into effect. Consequently, the objection that a special session was not held by the Bishops' Conference on that matter is really academic and without any practical value.

The representatives of the Church Abroad erroneously refer to the adoption of the Provisional Statute on the part of the American Metropolitanate in 1937 and to the corresponding action of the American bishops in order to substantiate their claims to full subordination of the American Metropolitanate to the Bishops' Synod Abroad. All articles that were not amended in the Provisional Statute of 1935 by the Sixth All American Sobor of 1937 were observed by the bishops of the American Metropolitanate. For instance, appointments of new bishops were always submitted for the approval of the Bishops' Synod in Karlovtsi.[32] It does not, however, follow that the authority of these organs was unconditionally recognized in all matters. The subordination was always limited. While participating in organs designed to coordinate the activity of Russian dioceses abroad, the American Metropolitanate preserved its own independence and the right of the All American Sobor to adopt final resolutions regarding the organizational problems of the Church without resorting to approval of another ecclesiastical authority.[33]

As to the objections against the abrogation of the resolutions of the Sixth All American Sobor in New York (1937) by the Seventh Sobor in Cleveland (1946), it must also be taken into consideration that there are sufficient grounds for holding the resolutions of the Sixth All American Sobor on the Provisional Statute simply invalid. As has been mentioned, the text of the Provisional Statute was adopted by the Bishops' Sobor in Karlovtsi in 1935. Since the Bishops' Sobor was the highest body of the Church Abroad, the approval of the Provisional Statute by the Bishops' Sobor in 1935 had already the force of law for all the members of the Karlovtsi jurisdiction. But the text of the Provisional Statute adopted in Karlovtsi in 1935 was for the American Metropolitanate only a draft which was to be presented to the All American Sobor for approval. As usual, this Sobor had to consist of bishops, priests and lay representatives of parishes of the American Metropolitanate. But the Sixth Sobor of 1937 was attended also by the bishops, priests and lay representatives of parishes which belonged to the Karlovtsi jurisdiction so that the question whether the Provisional Statute should be approved by the American Metropolitanate was decided not only by the members of the American Metropolitanate, but also by the votes of bishops, priests and parishioners of the Karlovtsi jurisdiction. Such irregular compositions of the Sobor undermines the validity of the adopted Provisional Statute. This violation of the rule concerning membership was of such importance that one can hold with good reason that if the Sobor had been attended by the members of the American Metropolitanate only, the decisions on merger would not have passed. The Provisional Statute, even with changes, was approved with only a minority of 105 votes out of 236 delegates in attendance at the session. Of the majority of 131 votes, 9 delegates voted against and 122 abstained from voting. During the discussions, the objections against the Provisional Statute were raised by the delegates of the American Metropolitanate only. Some of the delegates of the Metropolitanate could be found, of course, among those 105 who voted in favor of the Statute. But it is very difficult to find delegates of the Karlovtsi jurisdiction, the ardent proponents of merger, among those who voted against the Statute or who abstained. The Provisional Statute was adopted evidently not in accordance with the wishes of the majority of the delegates of the American Metropolitanate.

The peculiar composition of the Sixth All American Sobor was a consequence of the viewpoint of the Karlovtsi group that the union between the American Metropolitanate and the Russian Church Abroad had already been concluded by the agreement of the bishops. Therefore, immediately after that agreement, the Bishops' Sobor of the American Metropolitanate was attended also by the bishops of the Karlovtsi jurisdiction in America, and then this joint Bishops' Sobor convoked the All American Sobor also with the participation of representatives of both sides. All this was done before any acceptance of the Provisional Statute by the Sobor of the whole American Metropolitanate.

Longing for peace in the Church, the bishops of the American Metropolitanate made some concessions to the idea of the Karlovtsi Bishops that a union had already taken place. But they always insisted that the Provisional Statute had not been put into force completely and that the All American Sobor must be convened for its acceptance. It is true that even the introduction of delegates of the Karlovtsi jurisdiction into the Sixth All American Sobor of 1937 did not completely bring the effect desired by the Karlovtsi group. But the composition of the All American Sobor of 1937 was in any case totally irregular, so that a later American Sobor could not be deprived of the right to declare invalid the resolution of this Sixth All American Sobor.

7

The Church Abroad had a difficult time finding sound canonical substantiation for its authority. The Bishops' Sobor and Synod functioned as if they were supreme organs of an independent, self-governing, autocephalous Church. However, they encountered opposition to their supreme power over the entire Russian Diaspora not only on the part of the old Russian dioceses in Western Europe and in America but also by some Orthodox Local Churches. As early as 1927, Basil III, Patriarch of Constantinople, Meletios, Patriarch of Alexandria, and Chrysostomos, Archbishop of Athens, referred to the Karlovtsi Synod as an anticanonical institution which had no right to claim authority over all of the Russian parishes abroad.[34] Despite its failure to be recognized, the Church Abroad had resolved to exist "independent of the will and approval of any Local Church."[35]

A theoretical solution was found by claiming the Church Abroad as an "Integral part of the Russian Orthodox Church" that exists temporarily on an independent basis.[36] The adoption of this approach makes it superfluous to substantiate the canonicity of the foundation of a new autocephalous Church Abroad as well as its independence of other Local Churches. The Church Abroad considers itself part of the independent autocephalous Russian Church, founded a long time ago and recognized by all Local Churches; so it is claimed that the Church Abroad does not need to be founded or recognized as independent by other Local Churches. Therefore, it continues, only within the territory of a Local Church does the jurisdiction of the Bishops' Synod have to be recognized by that Church; outside the boundaries of Orthodox Local Churches, the bishops of the Church Abroad may perform divine services and rule the Church without any permission, protection, or supervision, inasmuch as there are Russian parishes in these areas.[37]

Though convenient, this theory is somewhat inade-quate, because there is little evidence that the Church Abroad is, in fact, part of the Russian Church and that it has "never broken canonical or spiritual communion with the Mother Church."[38] Being part of the Russian Church means belonging to it, being in administrative contact with it and, above all, recognizing its supreme authority. How then can dioceses which had never been incorporated into the Rus-sian Church consider themselves part of it? How can canon-ical communion endure after the Church Abroad has interrupted all relationships with the Moscow Patriarchate, and after Patriarchs Sergius and Alexis have suspended the bishops of the Synod Abroad? It follows that only spiritual communion remains, in view of the rupture of administra-tive relations with the Patriarch of Moscow.

But a question arises even as to spiritual communion. With whom does the communion exist? With the "Orthodox bishops of the Russian Church" who are not committed to the Moscow Patriarch, or with the "pious Russian people" who are custodians of piety in Russia, or with the "Church of the Catacombs?" In any case such communion has no canonical significance.

Moreover, any relationship is bilateral, and it is very difficult to establish that any Russians behind the Iron Curtain in the Soviet Union feel that the Church Abroad is connected with them, or that their feelings coincide with those of the Church Abroad. It is especially improper to speak of a "catacomb" or "underground" Church, Only an organized community of believers, united by a hierarchical authority capable of appointing and governing clergymen, can properly be called a Church. Small groups of Orthodox believers in the USSR, who do not recognize the authority of the Moscow Patriarchate and are, of necessity, disconnected from one another, can by no means be considered a Church.

Finally, it is noteworthy to mention that in the attempt to justify the independent existence of the Church Abroad, it is also argued that the Church Abroad is canonical because the Moscow Patriarchate is *not* canonical.[39] At first, the adherents of the Church Abroad noted the noncanonical character of only individual acts of the Moscow Patriarchate, and sometimes with good reason—for example, with respect to demands that both the clergy and the laity abroad be loyal to the government of the USSR. Now the entire Supreme Ecclesiastical Authority of the Moscow Patriarchate is declared to be uncanonical because it was organized with the help of the Soviet government and is acting in concert with it; and since the Soviet government is regarded as an apostate government whose authority is like that of anti-Christ, cooperation by the Moscow Patriarchate with it is considered equivalent to apostasy, to betraying Orthodoxy. Such "betrayal of Orthodoxy" divests, from the point of view of the adherents of the Church Abroad, any and all acts of the present-day Moscow Patriarchate of obligatory authority, that is, makes it uncanonical. From these premises the conclusion is drawn that the suspension of the members of the hierarchy of the Church Abroad, imposed by the Moscow Patriarchate, as well as all its other acts directed against the Church Abroad are not valid.

Moreover, in view of this uncanonicity of the Moscow Patriarchate, the Church Abroad bases its right to dissociate from Moscow on Canon 15 of the First-and-Second Council of 861. Canon 15, as well as Canons 13 and 14 of the same Council, as mentioned before, provide that any presbyter, bishop, or metropolitan shall be subject to deposition, if, under pretext of some charges against his superior, he should dare secede from communion with his bishop, metropolitan, or patriarch before the Council of Bishops has examined these charges. Canon 15, however, contains one complementary provision regarding the conditions under which the withdrawal from communion with the higher ecclesiastical authority is permitted without a preliminary examination of the charges made by the Council. This condition is interpreted in the book of Protopresbyter G. Grabbe, *The Truth About the Russian Church* (p. 139), in the sense that the penalty may be imposed only on those who cease to obey their church authority "without sufficient reasons"; but those who, prior to the examination of the case by the Council, withdraw from communion with their hierarchal superiors "on grounds of their actual betrayal of Orthodoxy" not only are not subject to any canonical penalty but "shall be deemed worthy to enjoy the honor, which befits them among Orthodox Christians."

However, according to the wording of Canon 15, this "honor" is to be accorded only those who withdraw from communion with their hierarchical superiors on account of some heresy condemned by the Holy Councils or Fathers—when a hierarch "is preaching the heresy publicly and teaching it barefacedly in church." In this unique case, secession is permitted before the verdict of the Council of Bishops has been rendered. This exception is made because the heretical character of the openly preached doctrine can be seen by all once this doctrine has been found to be heretical by a Holy Council. However, the followers of the Church Abroad do not present the least evidence of any heresy condemned by a Council which is openly preached by the Moscow Patriarchate. Under these conditions, the secession could not take place prior to the examination of the case by a Holy Council. The Council alone may establish that apostasy or a betrayal of Orthodoxy has actually occurred, whether "this apostasy" is worse than heresy or not,[40] and whether the charges against the hierarchy are well grounded. Hence the secession of the Church Abroad cannot be supported by Canon 15 of the First-and-Second Council of 861. As to the Bishops' Councils of the present Orthodox autocephalous Churches none considers the Moscow Patriarchate to be heretical.

References to this Canon 15 are all the more unfounded because it has no bearing on this case. As was indicated above in Chapter IV, Canon 15 is concerned only with the internal strife of the Church and not with the establishment of a new independent Church. The followers of the Church Abroad argue that it has the right to exist as an independent self-governing Church on the basis of this canon. But the charge of uncanonicity against the Moscow Patriarchate cannot endow the Church Abroad with a canonical character, so long as it has not fulfilled the requirements necessary for receiving the status of an independent and self-governing (that is, practically of an autocephalous) Church. As a result, this attempt to substantiate the canonicity of so extraordinary an organization as the Church Abroad does not have the desired effect, any more than do the other attempts discussed above.

The acceptance of something desired as a fact is very characteristic of the attitude assumed by the advocates of the Church Abroad. They consider their claims to certain rights as conferring these rights. The affirmation that the Church Abroad is an integral part of the Russian Church is just as much a gratuitous canonical fiction as the premises of this entire argumentation, that is, that the bishops who lost their dioceses were entitled to found a new independent Orthodox Church in areas that never belonged to their Mother Church, and that the Patriarchal Ukase of November 20, 1920, is the basic law of the Church Abroad. The very name, "Russian Orthodox Church Abroad," is a wish fulfillment inasmuch as it has never embraced all Russian dioceses and parishes abroad. Numerous Russian dioceses and parishes in Western Europe, America, China, Japan, and even Serbia, where the Church Abroad originated, do not now recognize the jurisdiction of the Bishops' Synod Abroad.

Owing to difficulties in finding canonical substantiations, canonical fictions are used. They are supported by references to a decision of a lower state court in a civil case concerning a single parish church. But this can never be a source of Orthodox Canon Law.

It is well to remember that neither fidelity to the teachings of the Orthodox Church, nor preservation of the Apostolic Succession, nor the piety of the clergy or laity of the Synodal Church are being considered here. Rather, we have only discussed the canonicity of its organization. The migration of the Orthodox faithful after the World Wars I and II assumed enormous proportions. The very scope of their movement itself raised very difficult canonical problems. However, since then, many years have passed. The sooner the abnormal canonical conditions are eliminated, the better for the whole Orthodox Church.

X

THE AMERICAN
METROPOLITANATE

The Russian Orthodox Church of America traces its origin from the Mission of the Russian Orthodox Church that arrived in Alaska in 1794. The Mission was made a diocese and eventually became the Russian Archdiocese of the Aleutian Islands and North America. Subsequently, this Archdiocese became the Russian Orthodox Greek Catholic Church of America or the American Metropolitanate. From its very inception, the Russian Church in America was designed "as a permanent church of the settled Orthodox population"[41] and not merely a church to take temporary pastoral care of Russian emigrés until their return to their homeland.

In determining the canonical status of the American Metropolitanate two periods must be distinguished: (1) from the arrival of the Russian Orthodox Mission in Alaska in 1794 to the Fourth All American Sobor in Detroit in 1924; (2) from 1924 to the present. During the first period the Russian parishes in America existed as part of the Russian Church. In the course of the second period, the Archdiocese of North America became an independent Local Church.

1

During the initial period, the American diocese was subordinate to the Holy Synod, as the dioceses in Russia were. The Holy Synod appointed bishops for America. The North

American Diocese was characterized by a much more active lay participation in ecclesiastical activities than other dioceses of the Russian Church. This was inherent in the American way of living that is based on the principles of self-government and the recognition of human rights. In 1907 the first American Convention or Sobor of the clergy and laity took place. Later on, by virtue of the decisions of the Moscow Sobor in 1917, the clergy and laity participated to an even larger degree in the life of the diocese. The Russian North American Diocese learned of these Moscow decisions with great joy and satisfaction. It became its basic task to put these resolutions into practice. According to the new Statute for Diocesan Administration adopted by the Moscow Sobor of 1917, Bishop Alexander Nemolovsky was elected as a ruling bishop at a convention of clergymen and laymen which took place in Cleveland in 1919; he was then approved by Moscow. Following the breaking off of normal relations with Moscow during the Russian Revolution, the North American Diocese was compelled to make independent decisions on problems of internal administration. The Ukase of Patriarch Tikhon of November 20, 1920, laid the canonical basis for further development of ecclesiastical self-government in America. Not being addressed to the parishes founded by the Bishops' Synod in Karlovtsi, this Ukase directly and obviously concerned the North American diocese, which was cut off from the Mother Church by political events.

However, it followed from Section 2 of the Patriarchal Ukase of November 20, 1920, that it was only applicable until such time as communication with the Supreme Church Administration in Moscow should be reestablished. That was the situation in 1924. At the end of 1923 in Russia the schismatic Synod of the Living Church dismissed from office Metropolitan Platon, who was openly critical of the Soviet regime, and immediately replaced him with a married priest, John Kedrovsky, who was "consecrated bishop" in Moscow. Although the Russian Archdiocese in America ignored this decision of the Synod of the Living Church, it had to accept the Ukase of Patriarch Tikhon, duly promulgated jointly with the Sacred Synod on January 16, 1924. By virtue of that Ukase, Metropolitan Platon was dismissed for having engaged in public acts of counterrevolution directed against the Soviet government. It was specified, however, that the Ukase was to take effect only as a new bishop could come to America and take over the office.

Both acts were clearly backed by the Soviet government, which was anxious to appoint a "loyal" clergyman as head of the American diocese so that the Church would become a tool in the hands of the Communist authorities. The new "conciliar" organization of the Church in America was seriously jeopardized. John Kedrovsky, the newly appointed Archbishop, had already brought suit in the Supreme Court of New York State to be given possession of St Nicholas Cathedral, which was held by Metropolitan Platon. The cautiously worded Ukase of Patriarch Tikhon concerning the suspension of Metropolitan Platon allowed the American diocese enough time to prepare itself for the coming Communist onslaught.

Consequently, the All American Sobor in Detroit later that year resolved to organize ecclesiastical life in America in a manner that would protect it from outside threats. The

Russian Orthodox Diocese in America was declared "a self-governing Church," being organized in accordance with the resolutions of the Moscow Sobor of 1917, and ruled by a locally elected Archbishop, the Bishops' Sobor, the Archbishop's Council (composed of elected representatives of the clergy and laity), and periodic Sobors of the entire American Church.[42] That system of self-government was made effective immediately. The American Church refused to obey the Ukase dismissing Metropolitan Platon. He was asked by the Sobor to head the new Church. Although Metropolitan Platon announced the interruption of all relationship with the Orthodox Church in the Soviet Union and proclaimed the Russian Orthodox Church in America temporarily "autonomous" in his Message of June 3, 1933, the American Metropolitanate had, in fact, existed as an independent Church since the proclamation in 1924 of Metropolitan Platon as the Head of the Church, which was in fact his election to a new office.

In response, the Acting Patriarchal Locum Tenens, Metropolitan Sergius, and his Sacred Synod declared the proclamation of the autonomy of the North American Diocese null and void, since it was made without the consent of the Moscow Patriarchate. The group around Metropolitan Platon was declared schismatic and Metropolitan Platon himself, as the initiator of the schism, was suspended; he was summoned before the Court of Bishops and charged with the violation of the 34th and 31st Canons of the Holy Apostles, the 14th and 15th Canons of the First-and-Second Council, and other similar canons. The decision of the Moscow Patriarchate of August 16, 1933, determined its subsequent attitude toward the American Metropolitanate. The Moscow Patriarchate continued to consider the American Archdiocese's proclamation that it was a "self-governing" Church a schism and an arbitrary secession of a diocese from the Central Authority of the entire Russian Church, and so suspended its hierarchy.

It follows, in this connection, that the essential problem in determining the canonical position of the American Metropolitanate is the problem of deciding whether the proclamation of its independence constituted a schismatic secession of a diocese from the entire Church or the establishment of a new self-governing Church. The stand taken by the Moscow Patriarchate is not surprising. The same viewpoint was defended by the Patriarch of Constantinople at the time the Russian Church proclaimed its independence in 1448 and the same thing happened with the Greek Church in 1833. But if we study the actions of the American Metropolitanate in 1924 at the time of the Detroit Sobor, we realize that it meets all the necessary requirements for the establishment of an independent Autocephalous Church:

(a) Its canonical origin is beyond any cavil since it was founded by the Russian Church as its foreign diocese, while its bishops were appointed by the Central Authority of the Russian Church of which it was an integral part.

(b) By 1924 the North American Metropolitanate had sufficiently matured for self-government. It had over 300 parishes, supported a Theological Seminary for the training of clergy, and had a number of affiliated organizations. It comprised three canonically appointed bishops, Bishop Stephen of Pittsburgh (appointed in 1916), Bishop Theophilus of Chicago (appointed in 1922) and Metropolitan Platon. A fourth bishop, Apollinarius, arrived from Yugoslavia shortly before the Detroit Sobor and attended all its sessions. In 1933, after Metropolitan Platon had severed all relations with the Moscow Patriarch in his Message of June 3, there were in addition to Metropolitan Platon, five more bishops: Archbishop Theophilus of San Francisco, Bishop Arsenius of Canada, Bishop Antonin of Baltimore, Bishop Leonty of Chicago and Bishop Benjamin of Pittsburgh.

(c) Finally, the American Metropolitanate was situated in an independent state, outside the territory of the Central Bodies of the Moscow Patriarchate. Patriarch Tikhon's Ukase of 1920 is also of significance for the Orthodox Church in America. On the basis of this Ukase, the American Metropolitanate had succeeded in expanding its activities to a degree to which it was entitled to claim autocephalous status.

According to the resolution of the Detroit Sobor, the American Church was organized as an independent "self-governing" Church. Of course, the head of an ordinary diocese cannot be appointed by a Local Sobor without the approval of Central Church Authority, and the Sobor comprising the clergy and the laity cannot decide ecclesiastical matters by their own authority only. In an ordinary diocese there is no such institution as the Sobor of Bishops, the latter being one of the highest Bodies of Administration. The intention of the Detroit Sobor to organize a new Church was especially revealed in its decision to inform all the Eastern Churches of the reorganization which had taken place (Article 3), evidently with the purpose of receiving their recognition of the independence of the American self-governing Church. True, this was referred to as "autonomy." But, that autonomy was always understood to comprehend the periodically convened American Sobors which acted as the supreme ecclesiastical authority able to elect Metropolitans, make laws, and fully regulate the life of the American Church. (*Cf.* Resolutions of the Seventh All American Sobor in Cleveland, 1946.) Metropolitan Gregory, who came to New York in 1947 as an emissary of the Patriarch of Moscow for negotiations, necessarily assumed in his letter of August 14, 1947, that these conditions demonstrated the desire to create an "autocephalous" instead of an "autonomous" administration.[43] But it is obvious that all other prerequisites for such autocephalous status were in existence in 1924, and, of course, to an even greater degree during the negotiations with Metropolitan Gregory in 1947.

2

Apart from the fact that the American Metropolitanate satisfied the three basic requirements for the founding of a Local Church, there were additional reasons that made it imperative to break away from the authority of Moscow and set up an independent Church administration in America. First was the desire to preserve intact the canonical order established by the Sacred Sobor of the Russian Church in 1917-18.

During the Soviet persecution, the conciliar structure of the Russian Church, established by the Moscow Sobor of 1917, was overthrown by a dictatorial, atheistic government. In keeping with the new conditions, the administration of the Church was rebuilt on a centralized basis. The

Communist government thought that it would be better able to direct the whole Church through a strong central Church authority. The Ukase of the Living Church in 1923, and then the Ukase of the Patriarchal Locum Tenens, Metropolitan Sergius, in 1933, ousting and replacing Metropolitan Platon, indicated that Moscow no longer wished to recognize the right of the North American Diocese to elect its own bishop, a right which was granted to every diocese by the Moscow Sobor of 1917. It was becoming clear that the administration of the Russian Church in America was now to be wholly subordinate to orders from Moscow, with the total elimination of conciliar cooperation with the American clergy and laity, which had been considered necessary by the Sobor of 1917.[44] This tendency to suppress the rising activity of the All American Sobor, and to put at the head of its administration only persons faithful to Soviet Moscow, became clearly evident later in the Ukase of Patriarch Alexis of February 16, 1945, concerning the reunification of the Russian Church in America with the Russian Patriarchal Church, and in the draft of the Statute of "the autonomous administration" of the Russian Orthodox Church in North America and Canada presented in 1947 by Metropolitan Gregory, the Ambassador of Patriarch Alexis.[45]

By these acts the Moscow Patriarch attempted to make subject to his own confirmation the election of any American Metropolitan, as well as the elections of the diocesan bishops. Patriarch Alexis, in his Ukase of February 16, 1945, recommended two candidates of his own (Metropolitan Benjamin and Archbishop Alexis) to the All American Sobor for election as Metropolitan. The Patriarch's Ukase went on to say that this imposed no limitation on the right of

the All American Sobor to nominate and elect its own candidate, but at the same time it was pointed out that the
Moscow Patriarchate had the canonical right to refuse to
confirm the candidate so elected for any reason whatsoever.
According to Metropolitan Gregory's Draft Statute, the
Metropolitan and the Bishops of the American Church were
subject to approval by the Moscow Patriarch and could be
deposed by him. This would make possible the gradual re-
placement of the entire episcopate; diocesan bishops would
all be replaced by bishops agreeable to Moscow. According
to the same draft, the decrees of the All American Sobor
would be subject to confirmation by the Bishops' Sobor,
and, by the same token, its entire activity would be subordinated to an episcopate faithful to Moscow.

In the same Ukase, Patriarch Alexis appointed Alexis,
Archbishop of Yaroslavl, chairman of the Sobor and sent
him to America. There was also a requirement of obedience
to all the directives of the Moscow Patriarch immediately.
The Draft Statute contained an implied threat to the
self-government of the Russian Church of America. Appointments and dismissals of members of the clergy could
be carried out and new restrictions imposed on the activity
of the Church administration. As a result, nothing would
have remained of the "full autonomy" for the recognition of
which the American Metropolitanate had been pleading.

The best indication of what the Moscow Patriarchate
wanted to achieve is the publication in 1954 of its
Polozheniye (Statute) on the Exarchate of the Moscow Patriarchate in America. By this "Statute," the Exarchate, with
its few parishes, was downgraded to the position of a simple

diocese, entirely subordinated to the Moscow Patriarch. The word "autonomy" is never once mentioned in the Statute.[46]

The American Metropolitanate actually found itself in the same position as its Russian Mother Church after the Florentine Union. From the Patriarch of Constantinople the Russian Church had wholeheartedly taken over the idea that the Orthodox Church rejected the supremacy of the Pope over all the local Churches, and that by his anti-canonical pretensions he had cut himself off from the Eastern Orthodox Patriarchates. But when in Florence, in 1439, the same Patriarch of Constantinople, jointly with other Eastern Patriarchs, had acknowledged the supremacy of the Pope over all the Local Churches and demanded that the Russian Church submit to the Pope as one of the Metropolitan districts of the Church of Constantinople, "the Russian Church," in the words of Patriarch Alexis, "saw the possibility of preserving the Orthodox faith only by remaining completely independent of the fluctuations of the Greek Church;"[47] and in this way it had preserved the traditional Church structure. So when, under growing pressure from the Communist government, the Moscow Patriarch, forced by circumstances to deviate from the decrees of the Moscow Sobor of 1917, continued to work to suppress the conciliar structure in America, then, to remain true to the legacy of the Russian Sobor of 1917, and to prevent the dissolution of the canonical structure based on its laws, the Russian Church in America had no alternative but to establish an administration that would be entirely independent of the Moscow Patriarchate.[48]

There was still another reason for declaring the independence of the American Metropolitanate, similar to the reasons for the break of the Russian Church with the Patriarchate of Constantinople. Both the *Kormchaya Kniga* (The Rudder) of 1653 and Patriarch Alexis referred to the submission of Constantinople to the "Moslem yoke" as a danger threatening the purity of Orthodoxy; it was particularly dangerous to have the appointment of the Moscow Metropolitan depend on the will of the Sultan. But today Communist pressure on the Russian Orthodox Church has proved to be even stronger than Moslem pressure on the Patriarchate of Constantinople had ever been. To restore and preserve its hierarchical structure, the Moscow Patriarchate has been compelled to support the foreign as well as the domestic policies of the Soviet government and to demand the same of its foreign dioceses. This was reflected in the ousting of Metropolitan Platon by the Moscow Patriarchate for his anti-Communist activity in Russia in the past, and especially in the demand of loyalty to the Soviet government from the entire foreign clergy. Whereas, in 1927, Metropolitan Sergius had demanded from clergymen abroad a written statement of their complete loyalty to the Soviet government in all their public activities,[49] Patriarch Alexis required in his Ukase of February 16, 1945, that the All American Sobor declare "in the name of the American Orthodox Church" that it would abstain from political activities against the USSR and that it give appropriate orders to all its parishes. In his earlier private letter of July 12, 1944, to the American Exarch of the Moscow Patriarch, Metropolitan Alexis (while still Locum Tenens) claimed that the demand for the utmost loyalty to the Soviet regime was "not a political, but an ecclesiastical condition."[50] This was designed to neutralize some of the citizens of the United States in the cold war between the Communist and the free world. But the carrying out of this demand would have put Orthodox Americans in a position that conflicted with their obligations as United States citizens to their homeland, and this alone would have been reason enough to repudiate it.[51]

One can only wonder how such an obviously political demand could be regarded as exclusively ecclesiastical. According to the Word of God the Church instructs its members to obey their own rulers (Rom 13:1-3; Titus 3:1). It never obliges them to obey the government of any other state. This demand of the Moscow Patriarchate would impose upon United States citizens the obligation to be loyal to an alien state—the USSR. This demand cannot possibly be considered either ecclesiastical or canonical. Members of the Russian Church in America, American citizens, had no choice but to repudiate it and to continue to obey their own Church authorities, who did not concur in this demand. The impossibility of fulfilling this demand was one of the reasons for the break in relations between the Russian Church in America and the Moscow Patriarchate, and for the proclamation of the former's full independence. In refusing to sign a loyalty oath toward the Soviet government, Metropolitan Platon considered it impossible and disastrous to tie in the existence of the Russian Church in America with the Russian Church within Soviet Russia, and he severed all relations with it (Message of Metropolitan Platon of June 3, 1933).

Embarrassed by the tactlessness of its demand for loyalty, in 1956 the Moscow Patriarchate announced that this demand "had been only temporary" and "had long since lost its force."[52] This is a belated, but obvious, admission of its impropriety. But the original demand for loyalty to Moscow was in full force both in 1933, under Metropolitan Platon, and in 1945-46, when the question of the recognition of the independence of the American Metropolitanate was being decided. In those years the American Metropolitanate had the right to draw its own conclusions from this demand, now lifted by the Moscow Patriarch himself.

However, the main goal, the neutralization of those clergy and laity who recognize the authority of the Patriarch of Moscow in the struggle between Communism and the free world, has now been attained without official loyalty oaths. In the Soviet Union, the Patriarch and the Sacred Synod cannot appoint a bishop, nor can a bishop appoint a priest, without the approval of the Soviet government whose organs control the activities of the Church. This consent is expressed in the registration of the seal and stamp of the new nominee.[53] The Moscow Patriarch and his Sacred Synod cannot appoint a bishop for America either, without the consent of the same organs. State control of Church activity is pervasive, particularly with regard to the foreign branches of the Church. Under these conditions a demand of loyalty proves to be unnecessary and superfluous.

Whereas, in the fifteenth century the Russian Church feared the subjection of its hierarchy to the Moslem power of the Sultan who controlled the appointment and activity of the Patriarch of Constantinople, the Russian Church in America has been even more aware of the danger to its hierarchy and clergy implicit in control of Church organs by the Soviet government.

3

By 1924, the American Metropolitanate had not only fulfilled three basic requirements to make it an Autocephalous Local Church, but there were additional weighty reasons inducing it to set up its own independent ecclesiastical administration. If it is recalled on what grounds the Russian Church, in the words employed by Patriarch Alexis at the Moscow Conference in 1948, "had the right" to autocephalous status in 1448, the obvious similarity between the situation of the American Metropolitanate and that of the Russian Church becomes immediately clear.

Both the Russian Church and the American Metropolitanate had once been part of one of the autocephalous Churches, and hence were of canonical origin. Both of them had enough parishes and bishops to carry on their own independent ecclesiastical administrations. Both were located in countries of vast territorial size and were completely independent of the country in which their Mother Church resided. Both were fighting to preserve the canonicity of their ecclesiastical structure as it had been transmitted to them by their Mother Church. And, finally, the Mother Churches, the Patriarchates of Constantinople and of Russia, became subject to the secular power of states which deprived them of the freedom necessary for the conduct of ecclesiastical affairs. The American Metropolitanate was entitled, therefore, to autocephalous status for the same reasons as those for which the Russian Church itself began its independent existence in 1448. Hence, the transformation of the American Metropolitanate into an independent administration, just as the installation in Moscow of a Metropolitan independent of Constantinople, was neither an illegal, arbitrary separation of a Metropolitan from his Patriarch (specified in Canons 13-15 of the Council of 861), nor a schism, but the lawful establishment of a new Local Church, warranted by the practice of the Orthodox Church.

In view of the obvious similarity between the situations of both Churches, it would be natural to expect that the Moscow patriarchate would recognize the independence of the Russian Church in America; the latter has long desired to win this recognition from its Mother Church. The Detroit Sobor of 1924 declared the Russian Orthodox Diocese in America a temporarily self-governing Church until the convocation of a Russian Sobor, which would draft definitive regulations for the conduct of relations between the Russian and American Churches.

When it became known that a Russian Church Sobor was to be held in 1945, the American Metropolitanate sent representatives who were empowered to petition for the recognition of "full autonomy." When the mission of the American delegates had failed, the Cleveland Sobor of 1946 addressed itself directly to the Moscow Patriarch with the request that he recognize the "full autonomy" of the American Metropolitanate and remain as its "spiritual father." But the Moscow Patriarch did not want to take any step that would lead to recognition of the independence of the Russian Church in America. This step could not be taken, on the one hand, because of an exaggerated idea of the rights of the Mother Church, and, on the other, because of the conditions under which the Church operated behind the Iron Curtain. It is easier, of course, for the Moscow Patriarchate to recognize the autocephalous status of the Orthodox Church in any country belonging to the Communist bloc (in Czechoslovakia, or Poland, for example) than to grant the same recognition to the Orthodox Church in America. Since it controls the foreign affairs of the Church, the government of the USSR need harbor no special misgivings in permitting the formation of an autocephalous church in any of the communist "republics." Alteration of the canonical status of these ecclesiastical bodies does not alter their subjection to control by a Communist government. A new and nominally independent Church in such countries can be kept within the general orbit of a Communist policy. Recognition of the autocephalous status of a Local Church in America, a free country, would not be a hollow gesture, however, but would mean the granting by Moscow of genuine ecclesiastical independence and self-government,[54] thereby cutting off all hope to control the activities of the American Church.

Recognizing the right of the American Metropolitanate to an autocephalous existence as a Local Church leaves unanswered the question whether, according to ecclesiastical practice, the American Metropolitanate could have unilaterally proclaimed itself an independent, self-governing Church at the Detroit Sobor in 1924, without the consent of the Russian Mother Church. We have already seen that the consent of the Mother Church cannot be considered canonically as an absolute precondition for the entry into communion with other Local Churches. We know also that the above question has been answered affirmatively by the Russian Church itself: It not only established its own independence by its own will and against the will of its Mother Church of Constantinople in 1448, but in 1948 invited the Heads and Representatives of all autocephalous Orthodox Churches to celebrate this act as the beginning of its autocephalous life. The question is also answered affirmatively by the Heads and Representatives of the autocephalous Churches who accepted this invitation and brought their good wishes to the Russian Church on the occasion of this anniversary. In view of this fact, the American Metropolitanate, having satisfied all the requirements for autocephalous status, had just as much right to proclaim Metropolitan Platon Head of the American Church in 1924 as the Russian Church itself had to place its reins of authority in the bands of Metropolitan Jonah in 1448. After the Moscow Conference of 1948, the Russian Church should be the last to object to the American Metropolitanate declaring itself independent. There are no grounds for the other autocephalous Churches to regard any differently the proclamation by the American Metropolitanate of its own independence than they do the same step taken by the Russian Church in 1448.

4

In spite of having every right to an independent existence, the Russian Orthodox Church of America does not enjoy official recognition of its independence by its Mother Church—the Moscow Patriarchate. In this respect it is canonically in the same position in which the Russian Church itself was for 140 years after the unauthorized election of Metropolitan Jonah to the Moscow See in 1448 and before Patriarchal dignity was conferred on it in 1589. After declaring its independence, the Moscow Metropolitanate no longer considered itself bound to follow the directives of the Patriarchate of Constantinople. Despite the interdict imposed on it by the Patriarch of Constantinople after the deposition of the Metropolitan Isidore, it appointed its own metropolitans and bishops, and its hierarchy went on administering ecclesiastical affairs and conducting Divine Services. The American Metropolitanate can do exactly the same and can ignore the directives of the Patriarchate of Moscow, whether in dismissing its bishops, suspending their right to perform Divine Services, or bringing them to trial. This hierarchy is the hierarchy of the American Metropolitanate and not of the Patriarchate of Moscow, so that it is not subject to any order originating in Moscow. When the Greek, Romanian and other Churches had separated from the Patriarchate of Constantinople and had severed their ties with it, they appointed their own hierarchy and administered their property independently of Constantinople. In this regard, the American Metropolitanate is following the usual course for newly formed Local Orthodox Churches.

In the words of A. Kartashev, "The Constantinople Interdict, for the sake of the prestige of the power of the Ecumenical Patriarch, was never formally lifted from the Russian Church. It lost its importance gradually with the passing of time, and at the moment when the Moscow Patriarchate was established in 1589 was not even recollected."[55] This interdict did not bar the Russian Church from coming into contact with the Eastern Patriarchates in the fifteenth century. Being autocephalous *de facto*, but not recognized as such *de jure*, it was still in canonical and liturgical communion with other autocephalous churches of that time.

Being self-governing and independent *de facto*, but not recognized *de jure* by other autocephalous Orthodox Churches, the Russian Orthodox Church of America is in liturgical and canonical communion with all the Patriarchates who have their dioceses in America, except the Churches "behind the Iron Curtain"—the Patriarchates of Moscow and Romania. The bishops and clergymen of the Russian Orthodox Church of America have been recognized as having been canonically appointed, and bishops from other Patriarchates do perform Divine Services with them regardless of the interdict imposed on them.

To bring to mind some of these cases:

On November 30, 1941, Macarius, the Brooklyn Bishop of the Russian Church in America, co-celebrated the Liturgy with Athenagoras, Archbishop of the Greek Archdiocese of North and South America, in the Greek Cathedral in New York. During the Liturgy they jointly consecrated a bishop of the American diocese of the Church of Constantinople.

During July 12-18, 1957, a world congress of Boy Scouts was held in Valley Forge. At this congress, Dimitri, Russian Archbishop of Philadelphia, performed the Liturgy in the open air jointly with Michael, Archbishop of the Greek Archdiocese.

On January 23, 1949, the last Liturgy in America before his departure for Constantinople was performed by the newly elected Ecumenical Patriarch Athenagoras in co-celebration with John (Shabovskoy), Bishop of San Francisco, representing the American Metropolitanate.

In December, 1960, John, Bishop of San Francisco performed with Athenagoras (Kokinakis), a bishop of the

Greek Archdiocese, the funeral service of Grand Duchess Olga Alexandrovna (Romanov) in Toronto, Canada. On this day the Liturgy was celebrated by Bishop John (Shahovskoy) and was attended by Bishop Athenagoras (Kokinakis), who received Communion inside the Altar.

The priests of the Russian Orthodox Church of America have often been invited by Athenagoras and Michael, the Heads of the Greek Archdiocese in America, to participate in Divine Services with them.

Also, the Archpriest Constantine Moraitakis attended as representative of Iakovos, the Greek Archbishop of North and South America, the consecration of Bishop Anatoly (Apostolov) by Leonty, Metropolitan of America and Canada, Iriney, Russian Archbishop of Boston, and Andrey, Metropolitan of the Bulgarian Church. The consecration took place in New York in the Holy Virgin Protection Pro-Cathedral of the American Metropolitanate on September 10, 1961.

The joint performance of Divine Services by clergymen of the Russian Orthodox Church of America with the bishops of the Syrian Antiochian Archdiocese and of the Serbian Diocese in America, and also by the clergymen of these dioceses with bishops and priests of the Russian Orthodox Church of America, is occasioned by their participation in the activity of St Vladimir's Orthodox Theological Seminary in New York. Having been founded as a graduate theological school of the Russian Orthodox Church of America, the Seminary soon became an inter-Orthodox institution, wherein members of various branches of the Orthodox Church in America receive a theological education.

At the beginning and at the end of the academic year, or when Seminary students are ordained, as well as on other occasions, the Russian priests on the teaching staff of the Seminary perform Divine Services with Antony (Bashir), Metropolitan of the Syrian-Antiochian Archdiocese or with Dionisije, Bishop of the Serbian Diocese in America. The Syrian-Antiochian and Serbian priests who are professors at St Vladimir's Seminary participate in Divine Services jointly with Metropolitan Leonty and other bishops of the Russian Orthodox Church of America. Sometimes this cooperation goes so far that students of the Seminary who do not belong to the jurisdiction of the Russian Orthodox Church of America are ordained by both bishops of their national jurisdiction and bishops of the Russian Orthodox Church of America. On September 21, 1960, P., a Serbian student of the Seminary, was ordained a deacon by Ireney, the Russian Archbishop of Boston, in the Holy Virgin Protection Cathedral of the Russian Church of America. Then, on October 23, 1960, the same student of the Seminary, Deacon P., was ordained a priest by the Serbian Bishop Dionisije in the St Sava Serbian Church in New York.

Notwithstanding its nonrecognition of the Russian Orthodox Church of America, however, even the Moscow Patriarchate acknowledges the validity of the Sacraments administered by it. In 1947, Archimandrite Dionisy (Diachenko) was elevated to the Episcopacy by three bishops of the Russian Orthodox Church in America: Theophilus, Leonty, and John, and later became one of the ruling bishops of this Church. In 1957, Alexis, Patriarch of Moscow, received Dionisy into the jurisdiction of the Russian Patriarchate with the rank of bishop, which order had been conferred on him by the Russian Orthodox Church of America, and soon he was elevated to the rank of Archbishop.

The existing liturgical communion is all the more precious for the Russian Orthodox Church of America as it persists in defiance of the interdiction on Divine Services imposed on the American bishops by the Patriarchate of Moscow in 1933, 1935, and 1947. This communion with the American representatives of the Ecumenical Patriarch, of the ancient Patriarchate of Antioch, and also of the Serbian Patriarchate is at the same time an expression of an actual recognition of the legitimacy of the American Metropolitanate.

In conclusion, it can be established that the Russian Orthodox Greek Catholic Church of America is now a self-governing independent Church, which enjoys practical rights equal to the rights of a Local autocephalous Church. It is not recognized *de jure* by other Local Orthodox Churches as an autocephalous Church, but it is recognized *de facto* by some of the oldest Patriarchates, with which it is in liturgical communion. It looks cheerfully to the future, recalling a similar and even longer road traveled by its Mother, the Russian Church.

5

Upon closer acquaintance with the history of individual Local Orthodox Churches, one is struck by the extreme individuality of the path traveled by them, the peculiarity of the tasks imposed on them by the course of events, the difficulties which they had to overcome, and the means employed for resolving these problems and overcoming these difficulties. At the beginning of the third decade of this century, the Russian Orthodox Church in America was confronted by the entirely unforeseen and extreme task of becoming the bearer of the legacy of the Sacred Sobor of the Russian Church of 1917-18 beyond the boundaries of Russia. It ruefully realized that the highest achievements of Russian canonical thought at this Sobor were repudiated by many members of the hierarchy for one reason or another, both in Russia proper and abroad. The Russian Orthodox Church in the Soviet Union, under the rule of the Communist government, simply had no opportunity to adhere to the principles proclaimed by the 1917 Moscow Sobor. The Russian Orthodox Church Abroad, founded by bishops who had fled from Communism, repudiated the conciliar cooperation of the clergy and laity which was established by the 1917 Sobor.

At the Detroit Sobor in 1924, the American Metropolitanate fully understood the peculiarity of its position and the sublimity of its mission. It decided to continue the work begun by the Russian Church before the Communist Revolution, and to effectuate in America what could not be done in Russia. The organization of the Church established by the Detroit Sobor is the church structure, in miniature, established by the Moscow Sobor in 1917. The Detroit Sobor also decreed that a detailed Statute of the new Church be prepared. This task was not completed for 30 years until the Ninth All American Sobor of 1955, which adopted the Statute of the Russian Orthodox Church of America.[56] The Statute is a detailed development of the basic principles established by the Detroit Sobor and brings the structure of the Church in America even closer to the structure of the Church as decreed by the 1917 Sobor.

According to the Statute of 1955, the highest legislative
and administrative organ is the All American Sobor. Like
the Sobor of the Russian Orthodox Church of 1917, it consists of bishops, clergymen, and laymen. All the bishops of
the Church are *ex officio* members of the All American
Sobor. Owing to the smaller size of the American Church in
comparison with the Russian Church, the multistage system
of elections of representatives of the clergy and the laity
from the dioceses was not needed. The Sobor consists of
representatives of parishes, and not of dioceses. The priests
of each parish are *ex officio* members of the Sobor. An equal
number of lay delegates of each parish is elected at a special
parish meeting (Article 1, Section 3). The principle of
parity of the clerical and lay delegates was borrowed from
the system of electing members to the Moscow Sobor. The
All American Sobor thus weaves all the parishes of the
Metropolitanate into an integral whole.

The participation of the clergy and the laity in the Sobor,
however, does not undermine the supremacy of the episcopate acknowledged by the Orthodox Church. The Sobor
makes decisions by majority vote of all its members present
at the meeting. But while voting with all the others, the bishops have powers that raise them above all the other members
of the Sobor. All the resolutions adopted by the Sobor must
be examined by the bishops at the end of each session. No
resolution is valid unless approved by the vote of at least a
majority of the bishops attending the Sobor (Article 1, Section 16). The instructions for the Moscow Sobor, approved
by the Russian Holy Synod on August 11, 1917, limited the
right of bishops to veto the decisions of the Sobor to cases
where they failed to conform to the Holy Scriptures, the

dogmas, the canons, or the Church traditions (Section 65). In keeping with the Statute of 1955, all the decisions of the Sobor, including those on economic matters, are to be submitted to the bishops for confirmation, and can be disapproved by them for any reason. The Statute stipulates that the bishops inform the Sobor of their approval or disapproval of the resolutions adopted by the Sobor, indicating their reasons in the event of rejection (Article 1, Section 16). This gives the clergy and the laity a chance to review their opinion, to discuss the problem anew with the bishops, and to find a solution acceptable to the bishops. The announcement by the bishops of their approval of the resolutions of the Sobor, after its concluding session, makes these resolutions into laws. They become binding on all the organs of the central and diocesan administration, all the parishes, all clergymen and laymen of the Russian Orthodox Church of America. They may be repealed or changed by the All American Sobor only.

The Bishops' Sobor is the highest hierarchical body invested with the broadest ecclesiastical power. As in other Orthodox Local Churches, leadership over the life of the Church is concentrated in its hands. Under the jurisdiction of the Bishops' Sobor are (a) all questions of doctrine, morals, and liturgical order, (b) decisions on the text of the Holy Scriptures and liturgical books, and (c) supervision of ecclesiastical arts and of religious education, of Church schools, colleges, and seminaries.

Whereas the All American Sobor must be convened every four years, the Bishops' Sobor may be convoked by the Metropolitan whenever necessary, and for all practical purposes, it becomes the organ that resolves the most important current problems of the general Church and diocesan administration. The Bishops' Sobor defines the boundaries of the dioceses, appoints the diocesan bishops, bestows all honors on bishops and higher honors on the regular and monastic clergy, resolves difficult problems arising in the administration of the diocesan bishops, receives clergymen into the Church, excommunicates clergymen and laymen from the Church, etc. (Article III, Section 3). In the system of Church administration, the Bishops' Sobor holds the same position as the Sacred Synod of 12 Bishops under the chairmanship of the Patriarch in keeping with the decrees of the Moscow Sobor of 1917. However, the Statute of 1955 also calls for the formation of a Bishops' Synod of four members for the examination of some of the less important current affairs (Article III, Sections 5-10). In relation to the more modest dimensions of the American Church as compared with the Russian Church, the American Bishops' Sobor is at the same time a general meeting of the Bishops of the whole Church.

In the Russian Orthodox Church of America the Metropolitan Council corresponds to the Supreme Ecclesiastical Council established by the Sobor of 1917. Like the Supreme Ecclesiastical Council, the Metropolitan Council is a mixed committee of representatives of the clergy and the laity. The Metropolitan Council consists of the Metropolitan as president, one bishop elected by the Bishops' Sobor, the senior priest of the Metropolitan Cathedral, five priests and five laymen elected by the All American Sobor. Like the Supreme Ecclesiastical Council, the Metropolitan Council is charged mostly with so-called "secular" affairs: economics, finance, the purchase, sale or encumbrance of

Church property, maintenance of institutions of charity and education, publication of books for propagation of the Orthodox faith, legal matters, etc. (Article IV, Section 1, 5).

The head of the Russian Orthodox Church in America is the Archbishop of New York, Metropolitan of all America and Canada. He represents the American Church in contacts with other Orthodox Churches, various religious organizations, and secular authorities. The Metropolitan holds an especially exalted position with respect to the other organs of the Church. He convokes and presides over the meetings of the All American Sobor, Bishops' Sobor, Bishops' Synod and Metropolitan Council; he gives brotherly advice to bishops and approves the decisions of the Metropolitan Council (Article II, Section 1, 2).

The high authority and reverence enjoyed by the Metropolitan in the Church stems from the way he is elected. Candidates for the Metropolitan See are elected by secret ballot by the All American Sobor (bishops, parish priests, and laymen together), but the final decision is made by the bishops attending the Sobor. To become a Metropolitan a candidate must be approved by a majority vote of the bishops (Article I, Section 20). This method of electing bishops, which dates from the second to fourth century, has now been revived in America. The same system of cooperation of clergy and laity is the basis of the structure of diocesan and parochial administration with the preservation of the full hierarchical power of the bishops and the leadership of the clergy in the life of the parish.

The building of Church life on principles of self-government is made easier in the United States by the fact that the United States Constitution gives all religious societies complete freedom of internal organization. The structure of the American Metropolitanate possesses some traits in common with that of the dioceses of other Orthodox Churches in America. According to the regulations of the American dioceses of the Church of Constantinople or of the Syrian Antiochian Church, the legislative authority over "secular" affairs is also vested in a diocesan Convention or Congress in which clergy and laity participate; the laity also participate actively in the administration of the parish jointly with the clergy. As for the general administration, clergy and laity take part in the election of the Head of the Church in many Patriarchates: Antioch, Serbia, Russia, Bulgaria, and Romania. In Communist countries, of course, freedom of elections is suppressed by the device of requiring government approval of the person elected. The Mixed Council of the clergy and the laity also exists in the Serbian, as well as some other autocephalous Churches. So, in following the decisions of the Moscow Sobor of 1917, the Russian Orthodox Church of America is acting the same as a number of other Orthodox Churches.

When the Patriarch of Moscow demanded that the American clergy and the All American Sobor make a declaration of loyalty to the Soviet government and of abstention from political activities against the USSR, this was interpreted by the American Metropolitanate as an attempt to subordinate the activity of the Church to the interests of a foreign power. It affronted their national feeling as American citizens and strengthened their conviction that the Russian Orthodox Church, in America, could preserve its canonical structure and its self-government only by becoming a Local American Church, in no way bound with the Soviet Union. This idea was particularly stressed in the reply of the Metropolitan Council to the Ukase by Patriarch Alexis of February 16, 1945. In defending the right of the American branch of the Russian Orthodox Church to establish its own independent church administration, the Metropolitan Council resolutely declared on July 10, 1945: "It is an American Church and an American Church it must continue to be." If Czechoslovakia or Poland can have small autocephalous Local Orthodox Churches, then America can organize an American Local Orthodox Church.[57]

While the Church of Constantinople, the Syrian-Antiochian, the Russian, the Serbian and Romanian Churches, all have their dioceses within the United States, as American dependencies of related Patriarchates whose headquarters lie outside of America, the Russian Orthodox Church of America is a Church of American citizens, which does not depend on any other ecclesiastical authority outside America and which has its supreme ruling bodies within the borders of the United States. During the 38 years of its independent existence (after the Detroit Sobor of 1924), the Russian Orthodox Church of America, unlike the American dioceses of other autocephalous Churches located abroad, became, in fact, the Local American Church. As a Local Church it freely accepts under its jurisdiction Orthodox clergymen and laymen who belong to Orthodox ecclesiastical groups in America which have no canonically established organization or canonically appointed hierarchy.

The growing Russian Orthodox Church of America has its own dioceses and parishes not only in the United States and Canada, but also in Argentina, Peru, and Venezuela. In 1960 the Romanian Orthodox Episcopate joined the Russian Church of America, though preserving the peculiarities of administration and language of the former. The Orthodox Church of Japan is also ruled by a bishop appointed by the Bishops' Sobor of the Russian Church of America.

Not a few obstacles were encountered by the Russian Orthodox Church of America in establishing an American Local Orthodox Church on the basis of the decrees of the Sacred Sobor of the Russian Church in 1917-18. In spite of all the difficulties caused by the Soviet-dominated Patriarchate of Moscow and the Bishops' Synod Abroad, it did not deviate from the last free decrees of its Russian Mother Church in 1917-18, but became the direct heir of its canonically creative work and continues onward upon its chosen path.

NOTES

1. Bogolepov, A., "On the 300th Anniversary of the *Kormchaya Kniga,*" *The Russian American Orthodox Messenger* (in Russian), no. 4 (New York, 1953), pp. 58, 59.

2. Kartashev, A., *The History of the Russian Church* (in Russian), vol. II (Paris, 1959), p. 44.

3. Duchich, N., *History of the Serbian Church* (in Serbian) (Belgrade, 1894), pp. 232-236.

4. *Acts of the Conference of the Heads and Representatives of the Autocephalous Orthodox Churches in Moscow, 1948* (in Russian), vol. I (Moscow, 1949), pp. 11-13.

5. Polsky, V. Rev. M., *Kanonicheskoye polozheniye Vysshey Tserkovnoy Vlasti v SSSR i Zagranitsey* (The Canonical Position of the Supreme Church Authority in the USSR and Abroad) (Jordanville, 1948), pp. 57-60.

6. Kartashev, A., *op. cit.*, vol. I, p. 376.

7. *Acts of the Conference of the Heads and Representatives of the Autocephalous Orthodox Churches in Moscow, 1948*, vol. I, p. 11 (Moscow, 1949) (in Russian).

8. *Zhurnal Moskovskoy Patriarchii* (Journal of the Moscow Patriarchate), No. 5, 1953, pp. 4-8.

9. Kartashev, A., *op. cit.*, vol. II, pp. 41-45 (in Russian).

10. Tomos of the Ecumenical Patriarch Meletios concerning the autonomy of the Church of Estonia, July 1923.

11. The Letter of His Holiness Athenagoras, Archbishop of Constantinople and Ecumenical Patriarch, to Cyril, the Metropolitan of Plovdiv, President of the Holy Synod of the Bulgarian Church, of April 25, 1953, and the answer of the Holy Synod of the Bulgarian Patriarchate of December 31, 1953, in *Tserkoven*

Vesnik, Sofia, January 22, 1954. The English translation was distributed at the Second Assembly of the World Council of Churches at Evanston, Illinois, USA.

12. *Edinaya Tserkov'* (One Church) no. 10-12, (New York, 1953), p. 17.

13. *Acts of the Conference of the Heads and Representatives of Autocephalous Orthodox Churches, 1948* (in Russian), vol. I (Moscow, 1949), pp. 18, 20, 23, 24, 29, 35.

14. Polsky, *op. cit.*, pp. 112, 118-120, 180.

15. *Ibid.*, p. 128.

16. Polsky, *op. cit.*, pp. 113, 114, 126. See also, Polsky, Very Rev. M., *Amerikanskaya Mitropoliya i Los-Angelossky process* (The American Metropolitanate and the Los Angeles Case) (Jordanville, 1940), pp. 20-22.

17. Polsky, *Kanonicheskoye polozheniye etc.*, p. 170. Grabbe, Very Rev. Georg, *Pravda o Russkoy Tserkvi na Rodine i za Rubezhom* (The Truth about the Russian Church at Home and Abroad) (Jordanville, 1961), pp. 209-211.

18. The text of the opinion (not reported in published opinions of the California courts) was printed by the Holy Trinity Monastery, Jordanville, NY, in the pamphlet *In the Superior Court of the State of California in and for the County of Los Angeles*, 1949. The citations have been taken from this text.

19. Polsky, *Amerikanskaya Mitropoliya etc.*, p. 24.

20. Polsky, *Kanonicheskoye polozheniye etc.*, pp. 114, 116, 119. *Russkaya Pravoslavnaya Tserkov v Severnoy Amerike* (The Russian Orthodox Church in North America) (Jordanville, 1955), pp. 6, 91-93, 159-167.

21. Andreev, I. M., *Kratky obzor istorii Russkoy Tserkvi ot revolutsii do nashikh dney* (A Short Survey of the History of the Russian Church since the Revolution until the Present Time) (Jordanville, 1951), pp. 92, 93, 99, 100.

22. Kohanik, Rev. P., "Canonicity and Arbitrariness," *The Russian American Orthodox Messenger*, November, 1955, pp. 173-176, (in Russian).

23. *Kanonicheskoye polozheniye Pravoslavnoy Russkoy Tserkvi zagranitsey* (The Canonical Position of the Orthodox Russian Church Abroad), edited by the Diocesan Administration of the West European Metropolitan District, Paris, 1927, pp. 12, 13, 50-52. Troitsky, S. V., *O Nepravde Karlovatskogo Raskola* (The Untruth of the Karlovtsy Schism) (Paris, 1960), pp. 123-125 (in Russian).

24. Schmemann, Rev. Prof. A., *Tserkov i tserkovnoye ustroystvo* (The Church and Her Structure) (Paris, 1949), pp. 7, 8.

25. Polsky, *Amerikanskaya Mitropoliya etc.*, p. 26.

26. The text of the provisional Statute of the Russian Orthodox Church Abroad—in the Collection *Tserkovniye zakony kasayushchiyesya Russkoy Pravoslavnoy Tserkvi zagranitsey* (Ecclesiastical Laws regarding the Russian Orthodox Church Abroad) (Jordanville, 1947), pp. 5-12.

27. Ibid.

28. *Acts of the Sixth All American Sobor of 1937* (in Russian), published by the Metropolitan Council, New York, p. 23.

29. *Acts of the Sixth All American Sobor of 1937*, pp. 28-31, 66-81. "Decisions of the All American Sobor of 1937," and "The Pastoral Letter of the Bishops' Sobor of the Russian Orthodox Church in America, October 12, 1937," *Russian American Orthodox Messenger* (October, 1937) (in Russian).

30. Polsky, *Kanonicheskoye polozheniye etc.*, pp. 163-164.

31. John, Bishop of Brooklyn, *Puti Amerikanskoy Mitropolii* (The Path of the American Metropolitanate) (New York, 1949), pp. 14, 15.

32. Polsky, *Amerikanskaya Mitropoliya etc.*, p. 7.

33. Bogolepov, A., "On the Occasion of the 35th Anniversary of the Sobor in Detroit" (in Russian), *The Russian American Orthodox Messenger* (1959), No. 12, pp. 82, 83.

34. Lomako, Rev. G., *Tserkovno-kanonicheskoye polozheniye russkago razseyaniya* (The Ecclesiastical-Canonical Position of the Russian Diaspora) (New York, 1950), pp. 9-19.

35. Polsky, *Kanonicheskoye polozheniye etc.*, p. 127.

36. "Message of the Bishops' Sobor of the Russian Orthodox Church Abroad" of December 15, 1951, quoted in Andreev, I. M., *Kratky obzor etc.*, pp. 171-175; "The Resolutions of the Bishops' Sobor of the Russian Orthodox Church Abroad" of October 19, 1956 (in Russian), *Pravoslavnaya Rus'* (Orthodox Russia) (1956), No. 21.

37. Polsky, *Kanonicheskoye polozheniye etc.*, p. 127.

38. Anastasius, Metropolitan, "Message of the Chairman of the Bishops' Synod," in *Ibid.* (October, 1945), p. 120.

39. Grabbe, Very Rev. Georg, *op. cit.*, pp. 105, 119, 136, 137, 140. Polsky, Very Rev. M., *Kanonicheskoye polozheniye*, pp. 85-89.

40. Grabbe, *op. cit.*, p. 116.

41. Schmemann, Alexander, "The Canonical Position of the Russian Orthodox Church of North America," *Year Book of the Russian Orthodox Greek Catholic Church* (1953), p. 22.

42. Chepeleff, Rev. John, "The Detroit All American Church Sobor of 1924," *The Russian Orthodox Calendar for 1955*, New York, pp. 169-172.

43. *Edinaya Tserkov'* (One Church), No. 3 (New York, 1947), p. 10.

44. Resolutions of the Sobor of the Russian Church on February 14, 20, and 22, 1918, concerning the Diocesan Administration, Sections 15, 16.

45. *Edinaya Tserkov'* (One Church), No. 3 (New York, 1947), p. 11. *The Russian Orthodox Messenger* (in Russian) (1945), No. 3.

46. Bogolepov, A., "New Statute of the American Exarchate of the Moscow Patriarchate"(in Russian), *The Russian American Orthodox Messenger,* No. 8 (1954).

47. *Acts of the Conference of the Heads and Representatives of the Autocephalous Orthodox Churches in Moscow, 1948* (in Russian), vol. I, p. 13.

48. *Acts of the All American Sobor in Detroit* (New York, 1925), pp. 7-12; Bogolepov, A., "On the Occasion of the 35th Anniversary of the Sobor in Detroit," *The Russian American Orthodox Messenger,* no. 2 (1960), pp. 24-25.

49. Letter of July 16/29, 1927, in Emhardt, W., *Religion in Soviet Russia* (1929), pp. 146-150.

50. Printed record on appeal in *Saint Nicholas Cathedral of the Russian Orthodox Church of North America against Kreshik et al.* in Court of Appeals of New York (7 NY 2d 191), fols. 5288-9.

51. Kochanik, Rev. P., "Criticism of the Latest Patriarchal Ukase" (in Russian), *The Russian American Orthodox Messenger*, March, 1948, pp. 37-40.

52. Statement by Metropolitan Nikolai, *Zhurnal Moskovskoy Patriarchii* (Journal of the Moscow Patriarchate), no. 1 (1956), p. 22.

53. Bogolepov, A., *The Statute of the Russian Orthodox Church of 1945* (New York, 1959), p. 7-8.

54. Bogolepov, A., *Tserkov' pod vlastiyu Kommunisma* (Church under Communism), Munich, 1958, pp. 166-167; Svitich, A., *Pravoslavnaya Tserkov' v Polshe i eye avtokefaliya* (The Orthodox Church in Poland and its Autocephaly) (Buenos Aires, 1959), pp. 47, 48, 205, 210, 213.

55. Kartashev, A., *op. cit.*, vol. I, p. 378 (in Russian).

56. *The Statute of the Russian Orthodox Greek Catholic Church of America*, Official text, English and Russian. Published by the Metropolitan Council (New York, 1956).

57. John, Bishop of San Francisco, "Do we carry on Negotiations with the Moscow Patriarchate?" (in Russian), *The Russian American Messenger* (October 1960), p. 166.

BIBLIOGRAPHY

I. Books And Articles

Anderson, Paul B., *People, Church and State in Modern Russia*, New York, 1944.

Andreev, I. M., *Kratky obzor istorii Russkoy Tserkvi ot revolutsii do nashikh dney* (A Short Survey of the History of the Russian Church since the Revolution until the Present Time), Jordanville, 1955.

Attwater, Donald, *The Christian Churches of the East*, vol. II, Milwaukee, 1948.

Antony, Bashir Archimandrite, *Studies in the Greek Church*.

Bogolepov, A. A., *Tserkov' pod vlastiyu kommunisma* (Church under Communism), Munich, 1958.

Bogolepov, A. A., *The Statute of the Russian Orthodox Church of 1945*, New York, 1959.

Bulgakov, Sergius, *The Orthodox Church*, London.

Callinikos, Rev. Constantine, *The History of the Orthodox Church*, Los Angeles, 1957.

Curtiss, John Shelton, *The Russian Church and the Soviet State*, Boston, 1953.

Deyaniya Soveshchaniya Glav i Predstaviteley Avtokefalnykh Pravoslavnykh Tserkvey 8-18 iyulya 1948 goda (Acts of the Conference of the Heads and Representatives of the Autocephalous Orthodox Churches, July 8-18, 1948), vols. I-II, Moscow, 1949.

Deyaniya Vseamerikanskago Tserkonago Sobora 1937 goda (Acts of the All American Church Sobor of 1937), New York, 1938.

Duchich, N., *Istorije Srpske Tsrkve* (History of the Serbian Church), Belgrade, 1894.

Emhardt, W. C., *Religion in Soviet Russia*, Milwaukee, 1929.

Grabbe, Very Rev. Georg, *Pravda o Russkoy Tserkvi na Rodine i za Rubezhom* (The Truth about the Russian Church at Home and Abroad), Jordanville, 1961.

Grigorieff, D., "Historical Background of Orthodoxy in America," *St Vladimir's Seminary Quarterly*, 1961, No. 1-2.

Heiler, F., *Uhrkirche und Ostkirche*, Munich, 1937.

Janin, R., *The Separated Eastern Churches*, London, 1933.

John, Bishop of Brooklyn, *Puti Amerikanskoy Mitropolii* (The Ways of the American Metropolitanate), New York, 1949.

Kanonicheskoye Polozhenie Pravoslavnoy Russkoy Tserkvi zagranitsey (The Canonical Position of the Orthodox Russian Church Abroad), ed. by Diocesan Administration of West European Metropolitan District, Paris, 1927.

Kartashev, A. V., *Ocherki po istorii Russkoy Tserkvi* (History of the Russian Church), vols. I and II, Paris, 1959.

Kidd, B., *The Church of Eastern Christendom*, London, 1927.

Lomako, Very Rev. G., *Tserkovno-kanonicheskoye Polozhenie Russkago Rasseyaniya* (The Canonical Position of the Russian Diaspora), New York, 1950.

Meyendorff, Jean, *L'Eglise Orthodoxe hier et aujourd'hui*, Paris, 1960.

Michael, Archbishop, *The Orthodox Church*, Brookline, Mass., 1952.

Onasch, Konrad, *Einführung in die Konfessionskunde der Orthodoxen Kirchen*, Berlin, 1962.

Ostrogorsky, G., *Geschichte des Byzantischen Staates*, Munich, 1940.

Patriarch Sergy i ego Dukhovnoye Nasledstvo (Patriarch Sergy and His Spiritual Heritage), ed. by Moscow Patriarchate, 1945.

Polsky, Very Rev. M., *Kanonicheskoye Polozhenie Vysshey Tserkovnoy Vlasti v SSSR i zagranitsey* (The Canonical Position of the Supreme Church Authority in the USSR and Abroad), Jordanville, 1948.

Polsky Very Rev. M., *Amerikanskaya Mitropoliya i Los-Angelossky process* (The American Metropolitanate and the Los Angeles Case), Jordanville, 1940.

Popan, F., and C. Draskovic, *Orthodoxie heute in Rumänien und Jugoslawien*, Vienna, 1960.

Postanovleniya Svyashchennogo Sobora v Detroite (Acts of the Sacred Sobor in Detroit), New York, 1924.

Russkaya Pravoslavnaya Tserkov (The Russian Orthodox Church), ed. by Moscow Patriarchate, 1958.

Russkaya Pravoslavnaya Tserkov' v Severnoy Amerike: Istoricheskaya spravka (The Russian Orthodox Church in North America: Historical Information), Jordanville, 1955.

Russky Pravoslavny Kalendar-Almanach (Russian Orthodox Calendar Almanac), New York, 1955.

Schmemann, Very Rev. A., *Tserkov' i tserkovnoye ustroystvo* (Church and Church Organization), Paris, 1949.

Schmemann, Very Rev. A., "The Canonical Position of the Russian Orthodox Church of North America," *Year Book of the Russian Orthodox Greek Catholic Church*, New York, 1953.

Schmemann, Very Rev. A., *Istorichesky put' pravoslaviya* (The Historical Way of Orthodoxy), New York, 1954.

Slijepcevic, D., *Die Bulgarische Orthodoxe Kirche 1944-1956*, Munich, 1957.

Spatharis, Avrilios, *The Ecumenical Patriarchate, a Many Century Old Institution*, Athens, 1959.

Spinka, Matthew, *The Church and the Russian Revolution*, New York, 1927.

Spinka, Matthew, *Christianity Confronts Communism*, New York, 1936.

Spinka, Matthew, *A History of Christianity in the Balkans*, Chicago, 1933.

Spinka, Matthew, *The Church in Soviet Russia*, New York, 1956.

Spuler, Bertold, *Die Gegenwartslage der Ostkirchen*, Wiesbaden, 1948.

Stratonov, I., *Russkaya Tserkovnaya Smuta* (Russian Ecclesiastical Dissension), Berlin, 1932.

Svitich, A., *Pravoslavnaya Tserkov' v Polshe i eye avtokefaliya* (The Orthodox Church in Poland and Its Autocephaly), Buenos Aires, 1959.

Timashev, N. S., *Religion in Soviet Russia*, London, 1943.

Timashev, N. S., *The Great Retreat*, New York, 1946.

Tobias, R., *Communist-Christian Encounter in East Europe*, Indianapolis, 1956.

Trempela, N., *Archai, kratisasai en ti anakiryxei tou avtokephalou*, Athens, 1957.

Troitsky, S. V., *O nepravde Karlovatskogo raskola* (Untruth of the Karlovtsy Schism), Paris, 1960.

Troitsky, S. V., "O tserkovnoy avtokefalii" (Ecclesiastical Autocephaly), *Zhurnal Moskovskoy Patriarkhii*, 1948, No. 7.

Troitsky, S. V., "Ecclesiologie Orthodoxe," *Messager de l'Exarchat du Patriarche Russe en Europe Occidentale*, 1951, No. 7-8.

Troitsky, S. V., "O edinstve Tserkvi" (The Unity of the Church), *Messager de l'Exarchat du Patriarche Russe en Europe Occidentale*, 1957, No. 26.

Upson, Very Rev. Stephen, *Orthodox Church History*, Brooklyn, 1954.

Vasiliev, A. A., *History of the Byzantine Empire*, Madison, 1952.

de Vries, Wilhelm, *Der Christliche Osten in Geschichte und Gegenwart*, Würzburg, 1951.

de Vries, Wilhelm, *Kirche und Staat in der Sowjetunion*, Munich, 1959.

Yubileyny Sbornik v pamyat' 150-letiya Russkoy Pravoslavnoy Tserkvi v Severnoy Amerike (150th Anniversary of the Russian Orthodox Church in North America), vols. I-II, New York, 1944-1945.

Zambonardi, Maffeus, *La Chiesa Autocefala Bulgara*, Gorizia, 1960.

Zoustis, B., *I Istoria tis Ellinikis Archiepiskopis Amerikis* (History of the Greek Archdiocese in America), New York, 1954.

II. Periodicals

The Eastern Church Quarterly, Ramsgate, England.

The Ecumenical Press Service, New York.

The Ecumenical Review, New York.

Edinaya Tserkov' (One Church), New York.

The Greek Orthodox Theological Review, Brookline, Mass.

Internationale Kirchliche Zeitschrift, Bern.

Irénikon, Amay, Chevetogne.

Istina, Boulogne-sur-Seine.

Messager de l'Exarcat du Patriarche Russe en Europe Occidentale, Paris.

Ostkirchliche Studien, Würzburg.

Pravoslavnaya Rus (Orthodox Russia), Jordanville.

Proche-Orient Chrétien, Jerusalem.

Russko-Amerikansky Pravoslavny Vestnik (The Russian American Orthodox Messenger), New York.

St Vladimir's Seminary Quarterly, New York.

The Word, New York.

Zhurnal Moskovskoy Patriarchii (Journal of the Moscow Patriarchate) Moscow.

The Seven Ecumenical Councils

1. Council of Nicaea—325 AD

2. Council of Constantinople—381 AD

3. Council of Ephesus—431 AD

4. Council of Chalcedon—451 AD

5. Council of Constantinople—553 AD

6. Council of Constantinople—680 AD

7. Council of Nicaea—787 AD